The Basics & Intricacies of Arabic Morphology

Joyce Åkesson

Pallas Athena

Lund

2010

The Basics & Intricacies of Arabic Morphology

2010 Pallas Athena Distribution, Skarpskyttevägen 10 A, 226 42 Lund, Sweden.

Book design by Joyce Åkesson

ISBN: 978-91-978954-0-8

PRINTED IN THE UNITED STATES OF AMERICA

ALSO BY JOYCE ÅKESSON

Majnūn Leyla: Poems about Passion, Pallas Athena Distribution, December 2009.

The Invitation, Pallas Athena Distribution, July 2009.

Love's Thrilling Dimensions, Pallas Athena Distribution, February 2009.

The Phonological Changes due to the Hamza and Weak Consonant in Arabic, Pallas Athena Distribution, April 2010.

A Study of the Assimilation and Substitution in Arabic, Pallas Athena Distribution, March 2010.

The Essentials of the Class of the Strong Verb in Arabic, Pallas Athena Distribution, January 2010

The Complexity of the Irregular Verbal and Nominal Forms & the Phonological Changes in Arabic, Pallas Athena Distribution, April 2009.

Arabic Morphology and Phonology: Based on the Marāḥ al-Arwāḥ by Aḥmad b. ᶜAlī b. Masᶜūd, Studies in Semitic Languages and Linguistics, Brill Academic Publishers, July 2001.

Aḥmad B. ᶜAlī B. Masᶜūd on Arabic Morphology, Marāḥ al-Arwāḥ: Part 1: The Strong Verb, Studia Orientalia Lundensia, Vol. 4, Brill Academic Publishers, October 1990.

ABBREVIATED TABLE OF CONTENTS

PREFACE

Despite the amount of material about Arabic grammar, phonology, and morphology, the need for a book combining an independent study in morphology with theoretical discussions is more than evident. This book fills that void by proposing an in-depth analysis of various morphological issues based on the seven classes of verbs and their nine derivatives. These classical classes are the strong verb, the doubled, the hamzated, the verb with 1st radical *w* or *y,* the verb with 2nd radical *w* or *y,* the verb with 3rd radical *w* or *y,* and the verb that is doubly weak. The nine derivatives are the perfect, imperfect, imperative, infinitive noun, active participle, passive participle, noun of time, noun of place and noun of instrument. The different sections introduce several paradigms of verbs, a carefully explored data and explicit information about the morphological structures and the various phonological changes that can affect them, such as the addition, transfer or elision of a vowel or letter, the assimilation of two letters and the substitution of one letter for another. The study pays also particular attention to the most representative works from the 8th century until our days.

1. THE CLASS OF THE STRONG VERB

The strong verb, *al-ṣaḥīḥ,* can be defined as the verb which has strong consonants as its three radicals, e.g. *ḍaraba.*

1.1. Form I conjugations and paradigms of the triliteral verb

The well-known conjugations of the triliteral can conveniently be divided into six ones:

1- *faᶜala yafᶜilu*, e.g. *ḍaraba yaḍribu* "to hit".

2- *faᶜala yafᶜulu*, e.g. *qatala yaqtulu* "to kill". There exist some anomalous cases as *faḍila yafḍulu* "to remain", which should have occurred formed according to this conjugation, namely *faḍala yafḍulu*, but which instead has *faḍila* in the perfect with the kasra given to the 2nd radical. Concerning it Sībawaihi, II, 240 remarks that it is an anomaly, and that preferably *faḍala yafḍulu* is more fit to be used according to the analogy. Other examples are *ḥadira yaḥḍuru* "to be present" and *naᶜima yanᶜamu* and *yanᶜumu* "to be affluent".

3- *faᶜila yafᶜalu,* e.g. *ᶜalima yaᶜlamu* "to know".

These first three conjugations are termed as *daᶜāʾim al-ʾabwāb* "the pillars of the conjugations" by Ibn Masᶜūd (Åkesson, *Ibn Masᶜūd* 50: fol. 3b) because of the variation of the vowels of their 2nd radical in the perfect and in the imperfect and because of their numerousness.

4- *faᶜala yafᶜalu*, e.g. *fataḥa yaftaḥu* "to open". As a general rule we can observe that when the 2nd or 3rd radical of the verb is a guttural consonant, namely *a ʾ, h, ᶜ, ḥ, ġ* or *ḫ,* the 2nd radical of the imperfect is vowelled by a fatḥa (cf. Sībawaihi, II, 270-272).

Some anomalies occur however in which the imperfect's vowel can be a fatḥa or a kasra, e.g. *naᶜaqa yanᶜaqu* or *yanᶜiqu* "to croak", or a fatḥa or a ḍamma, e.g. *salaḫa yaslaḫu* or *yasluḫu* "to flay". An anomalous verb which pertains to this conjugation is *rakana yarkanu* "to lean", which does not have any guttural consonant as a 2nd or 3rd radical. It could be a combination of two forms or of two dialectal varieties (cf. Lane, I, 1148).

5- *faᶜula yafᶜulu,* e.g. *karuma yakrumu* "to be generous". This conjugation denotes the quality and is intransitive.

6- *faᶜila yafᶜilu,* e.g. *ḥasiba yaḥsibu* "to assume". Vollers, *Volkssprache* 129 notes that Ibn ᶜAmir, Ḥamza and ᶜĀṣim read *yaḥsabu* instead of *yaḥsibu* from all the surs. of the Qurʾān.

The paradigm of *ḍaraba* in the perfect, active, is as follows:

	sing.	dual	pl.
1st	*ḍarab-tu*		*ḍarab-n(a)ā*
2nd masc.	*ḍarab-ta*	*ḍarab-tum(a)ā*	*ḍarab-tum*
2nd fem.	*ḍarab-ti*	*ḍarab-tum(a)ā*	*ḍarab-tunna*
3rd masc.	*ḍaraba*	*ḍarab(a)-ā*	*ḍarab(u)-ū*
3rd fem.	*ḍaraba-t*	*ḍaraba-t(a)ā*	*ḍarab-na*

<u>Its imperfect in the indicative, active, is the following:</u>

	sing.	dual	pl.
1st	*ʾaḍribu*		*naḍribu*
2nd masc.	*taḍribu*	*taḍrib(a)-āni*	*taḍrib(u)-ūna*
2nd fem.	*taḍrib(i)-īna*	*taḍrib(a)-āni*	*taḍrib-na*
3rd masc.	*yaḍribu*	*yaḍrib(a)-āni*	*yaḍrib(u)-ūna*
3rd fem.	*taḍribu*	*taḍrib(a)-āni*	*yaḍrib-na*

<u>Its imperfect in the indicative, subjunctive, is the following:</u>

	sing.	dual	pl.
1st	*ʾaḍriba*		*naḍriba*
2nd masc.	*taḍriba*	*taḍrib(a)-ā*	*taḍrib(u)-ū*
2nd fem.	*taḍrib(i)-ī*	*taḍrib(a)-ā*	*taḍrib-na*
3rd masc.	*yaḍriba*	*yaḍrib(a)-ā*	*yaḍrib(u)-ū*
3rd fem.	*taḍriba*	*taḍrib(a)-ā*	*yaḍrib-na*

Its imperfect in the indicative, jussive, is the following:

	sing.	dual	pl.
1st	*ʾaḍrib*		*naḍrib*
2nd masc.	*taḍrib*	*taḍrib(a)-ā*	*taḍrib(u)-ū*
2nd fem.	*taḍrib(i)-ī*	*taḍrib(a)-ā*	*taḍrib-na*
3rd masc.	*yaḍrib*	*yaḍrib(a)-ā*	*yaḍrib(u)-ū*
3rd fem.	*taḍrib*	*taḍrib(a)-ā*	*yaḍrib-na*

1.2.1 The derived forms and the paradigms of the triliteral

The common derived forms of the triliteral are the following:

1 - Form II *fa^{c}^{c}ala*, e.g. *qaṭṭa^{c}a* "to cut".

Its perfect in the indicative, active, is the following:

	sing.	dual	pl.
1st	*qaṭṭa^{c}-tu*		*qaṭṭa^{c}-n(a)ā*
2nd masc.	*qaṭṭa^{c}-ta*	*qaṭṭa^{c}-tum(a)ā*	*qaṭṭa^{c}-tum*
2nd fem.	*qaṭṭa^{c}-ti*	*qaṭṭa^{c}-tum(a)ā*	*qaṭṭa^{c}-tunna*
3rd masc.	*qaṭṭa^{c}a*	*qaṭṭa^{c}(a)-ā*	*qaṭṭa^{c}(u)-ū*
3rd fem.	*qaṭṭa^{c}a-t*	*qaṭṭa^{c}a-t(a)ā*	*qaṭṭa^{c}-na*

Its imperfect in the indicative, active, is the following:

	sing.	dual	pl.
1st	*ᵓuqaṭṭiᶜu*		*nuqaṭṭiᶜu*
2nd masc.	*tuqaṭṭiuᶜ*	*tuqaṭṭiᶜ(a)-āni*	*tuqaṭṭiᶜ(u)-ūna*
2nd fem.	*tuqaṭṭiᶜ(i)-īna*	*tuqaṭṭiᶜ(a)-āni*	*tuqaṭṭiᶜ-na*
3rd masc.	*yuqaṭṭiᶜu*	*yuqaṭṭiᶜ(a)-āni*	*yuqaṭṭiᶜ(u)-ūna*
3rd fem.	*tuqaṭṭiᶜu*	*tuqaṭṭiᶜ(a)-āni*	*yuqaṭṭiᶜ-na*

The meaning of Form II:

- It intensifies the meaning of the root.

- It can be similar to the groundform, e.g. *zaltuhu* and *zayyaltuhu* "I separated it". It can also have its meaning or the meaning of Form V, e.g. *badala, baddala* and *tabaddala* "to exchange". Some verbs are also intransitive.

- It makes causative transitive verbs, e.g. *ᶜalima* "to know" in the groundform, *ᶜallama* "to teach".

- It indicates the time when a thing is done, e.g. *ṣabbaḥnā massaynā wa-saḥḥarnā* "we went to find him in the morning, in the evening and at dawn".

- It has an estimative meaning, e.g. *ṣadaqa* "to believe" in the groundform, *ṣaddaqa* "to consider as sincere", and *kaḏiba* "to lie" in the groundform, *kaḏḏaba* "to consider as a liar".

- It makes someone or something do a thing, e.g. *kattaba* "to make someone write".

- It is derived from nouns and expresses their meanings, e.g. *ḫubzun* "bread", *ḫabbaza* "to bake bread".

- It expresses the negation of the idea existing in the groundform, e.g. *fazi*ᶜ*a* "to fear", *fazza*ᶜ*a* "to deliver from fear".

- It expresses a blessing, e.g. *saqqaytuhu wa-ra*ᶜᶜ*aytuhu* " I said to him: *saqyan wa-ra*ᶜ*yan* "May God preserve you and give you rain".

- It denotes a movement from one place to another, e.g. *šarraqa* "to go to the Orient", *ġarraba* "to go to the Occident" and *kawwafa* "to go to al-Kūfa".

- It denotes becoming its root, e.g. ᶜ*ağğazati l-mar*ᵓ*atu* "the woman became a ᶜ*ağūzun* "an old woman".

2 - Form III *fāᶜala*, e.g. *qātala* "to fight".

Its perfect in the indicative, active, is the following:

	sing.	dual	pl.
1st	*qātal-tu*		*qātal-n(a)ā*
2nd masc.	*qātal-ta*	*qātal-tum(a)ā*	*qātal-tum*
2nd fem.	*qātal-ti*	*qātal-tum(a)ā*	*qātal-tunna*
3rd masc.	*qātala*	*qātal(a)-ā*	*qātal(u)-ū*
3rd fem.	*qātala-t*	*qātala-t(a)ā*	*qātal-na*

Its imperfect in the indicative, active, is the following:

	sing.	dual	pl.
1st	*ᵓuqātilu*		*nuqātilu*
2nd masc.	*tuqātilu*	*tuqātil(a)-āni*	*tuqātil(u)-ūna*
2nd fem.	*tuqātil(i)-īna*	*tuqātil(a)-āni*	*tuqātil-na*
3rd masc.	*yuqātilu*	*yuqātil(a)-āni*	*yuqātil(u)-ūna*
3rd fem.	*tuqātilu*	*tuqātil(a)-āni*	*yuqātil-na*

The meaning of Form III:

- It denotes the idea of reciprocity, e.g. *ḍārabtuhu* "I hit him and he hit me".

- It denotes the idea of rivality, e.g. *šarufa* "to be high-ranking" in the groundform, *šārafa* "to vie for precedence in honor or nobility".

- It denotes enduring the action of the groundform, e.g. *qasā* (with final *alif mamdūda)* "to be harsh" and *qāsā* (with final *alif maqṣūra)* "to suffer".

- It comprehends the meaning of the prepositions, e.g. *ǧalasa ᶜinda l-sulṭāni and ǧālasa l-sulṭāna* "he sat near the sultan".

- It can be similar to the groundform, e.g. *safara* and *sāfara* "to go forth to journey".

- It can be similar to Form II *faᶜᶜala,* e.g. *ḍāᶜaftu* "I doubled [the thing]", like *ḍaᶜᶜaftuhu.*

- It can be similar to Form IV *ᵓafᶜala,* e.g. *rāᶜinā samᶜaka* "make your ear to be possessed of mindfulness for us", like *ᵓarᶜinā.*

3 - Form IV *ᵓafᶜala*, e.g. *ᵓakrama* "to honour".

Its perfect in the indicative, active, is the following:

	sing.	dual	pl.
1st	*ᵓakram-tu*		*ᵓakram-n(a)ā*
2nd masc.	*ᵓakram-ta*	*ᵓakram(a)-ā*	*ᵓakram-tum*
2nd fem.	*ᵓakram-ti*	*ᵓakram-tum(a)ā*	*ᵓakram-tunna*
3rd masc.	*ᵓakrama*	*ᵓakram(a)-ā*	*ᵓakram(u)-ū*
3rd fem.	*ᵓakrama-t*	*ᵓakrama-t(a)ā*	*ᵓakram-na*

Its imperfect in the indicative, active, is the following:

	sing.	dual	pl.
1st	*ᵓuᵓakrimu*		*nuᵓakrimu*
2nd masc.	*tuᵓakrimu*	*tuᵓakrim(a)-āni*	*tuᵓakrim(u)-ūna*
2nd fem.	*tuᵓakrim(i)-īna*	*tuᵓakrim(a)-āni*	*tuᵓakrim-na*
3rd masc.	*yuᵓakrimu*	*yuᵓakrim(a)-āni*	*yuᵓakrim(u)-ūna*
3rd fem.	*tuᵓakrimu*	*tuᵓakrim(a)-āni*	*yuᵓakrim-na*

The meaning of Form IV:

- It can be formed from nouns, e.g. *ᵓaqfara* "to become a desert" from *qafrun* "desert", *ᵓarāba* "to incur suspicion" from *raybun* "suspicion".

- It denotes entering a place or time, e.g. *ʾanǧada* "to enter Naǧd", *ʾaǧbala* "to enter the mountain" and *ʾaṣbaḥa* "to enter upon the morning".

- It denotes moving from one place to another, e.g. *ʾaḥǧaza* "he went to al-Ḥiǧāz" and *ʾaġraba* "he went to the Occident".

- It denotes finding a quality in the object, e.g. *ʾaḥmadtuhu* "I found him such as to be praised".

- It denotes exposing, e.g. *ʾaqtaltuhu* "I exposed him to slaughter" and *ʾabaʿtuhu* "I exposed him to sale".

- It denotes depriving, e.g. *ʾaškaytuhu* "I removed his complaint".

- It denotes negating the groundform, e.g. *šaqā* (with final *alif maqṣūra)* "to be cured" and *ʾašqā* (with final *alif maqṣūra)* "not to be cured".

4 - Form V *tafaʿʿala, e.g. tafaḍḍala* "to deign".

Its perfect in the indicative, active, is the following:

	sing.	dual	pl.
1st	*tafaḍḍal-tu*		*tafaḍḍal-n(a)ā*
2nd masc.	*tafaḍḍal-ta*	*tafaḍḍal-tum(a)ā*	*tafaḍḍal-tum*
2nd fem.	*tafaḍḍal-ti*	*tafaḍḍal-tum(a)ā*	*tafaḍḍal-tunna*
3rd masc.	*tafaḍḍala*	*tafaḍḍal(a)-ā*	*tafaḍḍal(u)-ū*
3rd fem.	*tafaḍḍala-t*	*tafaḍḍala-t(a)ā*	*tafaḍḍal-na*

Its imperfect in the indicative, active, is the following:

	sing.	dual	pl.
1st	*ᵓatafaḍḍalu*		*natafaḍḍalu*
2nd masc.	*tatafaḍḍalu*	*tatafaḍḍal(a)-āni*	*tatafaḍḍal(u)-ūn*
2nd fem.	*tatafaḍḍal(i)-īna*	*tatfaḍḍal(a)-āni*	*tatafaḍḍal-na*
3rd masc.	*yatafaḍḍalu*	*yatafaḍḍal(a)-āni*	*yatafaḍḍal(u)-ūna*
3rd fem.	*tatafaḍḍalu*	*tatafaḍḍal(a)-āni*	*yatafaḍḍal-na*

The meaning of Form V:

- It is the reflexive to Form II *faᶜᶜala,* e.g. *kassartuhu fa-takassara* "I broke it in pieces and it broke in pieces".

- It denotes affecting, e.g. *tašağğaᶜa* "he encouraged himself", or endeavouring to acquire, e.g. *taḥallama* "he endeavoured to acquire forbearance".

- It is similar to Form X *ᵓistafᶜala,* with its two meanings of believing and requiring, e.g. *takabbara* "he believed himself to be great" and *tabayyanahu* "he sought the settlement and manifestation of it.

- It denotes a repeated action that occurs progressively in time, e.g. *tağarraᶜahu* "he swallowed it in successive gulps".

- It denotes taking for oneself, e.g. *tadayyartu l-makāna* "I took the place for an abode" and *tawassadtu l-turāba* "I took the dust for a pillow".

- It denotes associating with a religion, a sect, a nation or a tribe, e.g. *tanaṣṣara* "to become a Christian", *tahawwada* "to become a Jew", *taqayyasa* "to associate with the Qaisī tribe", *taᶜarraba* "to become an Arab" and *tašaᵓᵓama* "to become a Syrian".

- It denotes abstaining from the action of the groundform, e.g. *tahağğada* "to stay awake at night" and *taḥawwaba* "to abstain from sin".

5 - Form VI *tafāᶜala*, e.g. *taḍāraba* "to strike".

Its perfect in the indicative, active, is the following:

	sing.	dual	pl.
1st	*taḍārab -tu*		*taḍārab-n(a)ā*
2nd masc.	*taḍārab-ta*	*taḍārab-tum(a)ā*	*taḍārab-tum*
2nd fem.	*taḍārab-ti*	*taḍārab-tum(a)ā*	*taḍārab-tunna*
3rd masc.	*taḍāraba*	*taḍārab(a)-ā*	*taḍārab(u)-ū*
3rd fem.	*taḍāraba-t*	*taḍāraba-t(a)ā*	*taḍārab-na*

Its imperfect in the indicative, active, is the following:

	sing.	dual	pl.
1st	*ᵓataḍārabu*		*nataḍārabu*
2nd masc.	*tataḍārabu*	*tataḍārab(a)-āni*	*tataḍārab(u)-ūna*
2nd fem.	*tataḍārab(i)-īna*	*tatfaḍḍal(a)-āni*	*tataḍārab-na*
3rd masc.	*yatḍārabu*	*yataḍārab(a)-āni*	*yataḍārab(u)-ūna*
3rd fem.	*tataḍārabu*	*tataḍārab(a)-āni*	*yataḍārab-na*

The meaning of Form VI:

- It denotes an action done by two and more, e.g. taḍārabā "they both fought together" and taḍārabū "they fought together".

- It is similar to the groundform, e.g. *tawānaytu* "I flagged in the matter".

- It is the reflexive of Form II *faᶜᶜala,* e.g. *ᶜaẓẓamtuhu fa-taᶜaẓẓama* "I glorified him and he was glorified".

- It is the reflexive of Form III *fāᶜala,* e.g. *bāᶜadtuhu fa-tabāᶜada* "I made him to remove to a distance, and he removed to it".

- It is similar to Form VIII *ᵓiftaᶜala,* e.g. *taḍārabū* and ᵓiḍṭarabū "they hit each other", and *taqātalū* and *ᵓiqtatalū* "they killed each other".

- It denotes stimulating an action or a state, e.g. *taǧāhaltu* "I feigned to be ignorant".

6 - Form VII *ʾinfaʿala,* e.g. *ʾinṣarafa* "to depart".

Its perfect in the indicative, active, is the following:

	sing.	dual	pl.
1st	*ʾinṣaraf-tu*		*ʾinṣaraf-n(a)ā*
2nd masc.	*ʾinṣaraf-ta*	*ʾinṣaraf-tum(a)ā*	*ʾinṣaraf-tum*
2nd fem.	*ʾinṣaraf-ti*	*ʾinṣaraf-tum(a)ā*	*ʾinṣaraf-tunna*
3rd masc.	*ʾinṣarafa*	*ʾinṣaraf(a)-ā*	*ʾinṣaraf(u)-ū*
3rd fem.	*ʾinṣarafa-t*	*ʾinṣarafa-t(a)ā*	*ʾinṣaraf-na*

Its imperfect in the indicative, active, is the following:

	sing.	dual	pl.
1st	*ʾanṣarifu*		*nanṣarifu*
2nd masc.	*tanṣarifu*	*tanṣarif(a]-āni*	*tanṣarif(u)-ūna*
2nd fem.	*tanṣarif(i)-īna*	*tanṣarif(a)-āni*	*tanṣarif-na*
3rd masc.	*yanṣarifu*	*yanṣarif(a)-āni*	*yanṣarif(u)-ūna*
3rd fem.	*tanṣarifu*	*tanṣarif(a)-āni*	*yanṣarif-na*

The meaning of Form VII:

- It is the passive of the groundform *faᶜala,* e.g. *kasartuhu fa-nkasara* "I broke it and it broke".

7 - Form VIII *ʾiftaᶜala,* e.g. *ʾiḥtaqara* "to despise".

Its perfect in the indicative, active, is the following:

	sing.	dual	pl.
1st	*ʾiḥtaqar-tu*		*ʾiḥtaqar-n(a)ā*
2nd masc.	*ʾiḥtaqar-ta*	*ʾiḥtaqar-tum(a)ā*	*ʾiḥtaqar-tum*
2nd fem.	*ʾiḥtaqar-ti*	*ʾiḥtaqar-tum(a)ā*	*ʾiḥtaqar-tunna*
3rd masc.	*ʾiḥtaqara*	*ʾiḥtaqar(a)-ā*	*ʾiḥtaqar(u)-ū*
3rd fem.	*ʾiḥtaqara-t*	*ʾiḥtaqara-t(a)ā*	*ʾiḥtaqar-na*

Its imperfect in the indicative, active, is the following:

	sing.	dual	pl.
1st	*ʾaḥtaqiru*		*naḥtaqiru*
2nd masc.	*taḥtaqiru*	*taḥtaqir(a)-āni*	*taḥtaqir(u)-ūna*
2nd fem.	*taḥtaqir(i)-īna*	*taḥtaqir(a)-āni*	*taḥtaqir-na*
3rd masc.	*yaḥtaqiru*	*yaḥtaqir(a)-āni*	*yaḥtaqir(u)-ūna*
3rd fem.	*taḥtaqiru*	*taḥtaqir(a)-āni*	*yaḥtaqir-na*

The meaning of Form VIII:

- It is similar to the groundform, e.g. *kasaba* and *ʾiktasaba* "to obtain".

- It is the reflexive of the groundform, e.g. *samiᶜa* "to hear" and *ʾistamaᶜa* "to listen to" and *ǧamaᶜa* "to collect" and *ʾiǧtamaᶜa* "to collect themselves".

- It is similar to Form VI *tafāᶜala*, e.g. *taqātalū* "they killed each other" and *ʾiqtatalū* and *taǧāwarū* and *ʾiǧtawarū* "they became mutual neighbours".

- It is similar to Form VII *ʾinfaᶜala,* e.g. *ġamamtuhu fa-ġtamma wa-nġamma* "I grieved him and he grieved".

- It denotes making for oneself, e.g. *ʾištawā* "to roast meat".

8 - Form IX *ʾifᶜalla,* e.g. *ʾiḥmarra* "to be red".

Its perfect in the indicative, active, is the following:

	sing.	dual	pl.
1st	*ʾiḥmarar-tu*		*ʾiḥmarar-n(a)ā*
2nd masc.	*ʾiḥmararar-ta*	*ʾiḥmarar-tum(a)ā*	*ʾiḥmarar-tum*
2nd fem.	*ʾiḥmarar-ti*	*ʾiḥmarar-tum(a)ā*	*ʾiḥmarar-tunna*
3rd masc.	*ʾiḥmarra*	*ʾiḥmarr(a)-ā*	*ʾiḥmarr(u)-ū*
3rd fem.	*ʾiḥmarra-t*	*ʾiḥmarra-t(a)ā*	*ʾiḥmarar-na*

Its imperfect in the indicative, active, is the following:

	sing.	dual	pl.
1st	*ʾaḥmarru*		*naḥmarru*
2nd masc.	*taḥmarru*	*taḥmarr(a)-āni*	*taḥmarr(u)-ūna*
2nd fem.	*taḥmarr(i)-īna*	*taḥmarr(a)-āni*	*taḥmarir-na*
3rd masc.	*yaḥmarru*	*yaḥmarr(a)-āni*	*yamarr(u)-ūna*
3rd fem.	*taḥmarru*	*taḥmarr(a)-āni*	*yaḥmarir-na*

The meaning of Form IX:

- It is used for permanent colours or defects.

9 - Form X *ʾistafᶜala,* e.g. *ʾistaḫraǧa* "to remove".

Its perfect in the indicative, active, is the following:

	sing.	dual	pl.
1st	*ʾistaḫraǧ-tu*		*ʾistaḫraǧ-n(a)ā*
2nd masc.	*ʾistaḫraǧ-ta*	*ʾistaḫraǧ-tum(a)ā*	*ʾistaḫraǧ-tum*
2nd fem.	*ʾistaḫraǧ-ti*	*ʾistaḫraǧ-tum(a)ā*	*ʾistaḫraǧ-tunna*
3rd masc.	*ʾistaḫraǧa*	*ʾistaḫraǧ(a)-ā*	*ʾistaḫraǧ(u)-ū*
3rd fem.	*ʾistaḫraǧa-t*	*ʾistaḫraǧa-t(a)ā*	*ʾistaḫraǧ-na*

Its imperfect in the indicative, active, is the following:

	sing.	dual	pl.
1st	*ʾastaḫriğu*		*nastaḫriğu*
2nd masc.	*tastaḫriğu*	*tastaḫriğ(a)-āni*	*tastaḫriğ(u)-ūna*
2nd fem.	*tastaḫriğ(i)-īna*	*tastaḫriğ(a)-āni*	*tastaḫriğ-na*
3rd masc.	*yastaḫriğu*	*yastaḫriğ(a)-āni*	*yastaḫriğ(u)-ūna*
3rd fem.	*tastaḫriğu*	*tastaḫriğ(a)-āni*	*yastaḫriğ-na*

The meaning of Form X:

- It is similar to the groundform, e.g. *qarra* and *ʾistaqarra* "to rest".

- It denotes the request of the act, e.g. *ʾistaᶜmalahu* "he required his working".

- It denotes becoming transmuted, e.g. *ʾistaḥğara l-ṭīnu* "the clay became stone".

- It denotes finding someone to be of a certain quality, e.g. *ʾistaᶜẓamtuhu* "I found him to be grand".

- It denotes appointing someone for a position, e.g. *ʾistawzara* "to appoint one as a minister".

10 - Form XI *ʾifʿālla,* e.g. *ʾiḥmārra* "to be very red".

The meaning of Form XI:

- It intensifies Form IX *ʾifʿalla.*

11- Form XII *ʾifʿawʿala,* e.g. *ʾiʿšawšaba* "to cover with luxuriant herbage".

The meaning of Form XII:

- It denotes intensity.

12- Form XIII *ʾifʿawwala,* e.g. *ʾiǧlawwada* "to last long".

The two more anomalous forms are the following:

13- Form XIV: *ʾifʿanlala,* e.g. *ʾisḥankaka* "to be dark".

14- Form XV *ʾifʿanlā* e.g. *ʾiḥbanṭā* "to be swollen or filled with rage".

1.3. The forms of the quadriliteral

The strong verb's quadriliteral can generally be:

1- a combination of well-known syllables in common expressions, e.g. *basmala* "to say *bi-smi l-lāhi* 'in the name of God'".

2- a repeated biliteral root expressing a sound or a movement, e.g. *zalzala* "to shake".

3- a triliteral verb that has been developed through the insertion of one augment resulting in a form that is identical in its structure to Form I *faᶜlala*, .e.g. *zaḥlafa* "to roll along" from *zaḥafa* "to advance slowly", or the insertion of two augments resulting in forms that are coordinated to Form II *tafaᶜlala,* e.g. *tağalbaba* "to put on a *ğilbābun* 'garment'" from *ğalaba* "to bring", or more than two augments resulting in forms that are coordinated to Form III *ᵓifᶜanlala.*

The development of the triliteral verb into being of four, five, or six segments, is named according to de Sacy, I, 125 *al-mulḥaqāt bi-l-rubāᶜī* "commensurable to be coordinated with the quadriliteral".

4- formed from foreign words of more than three segments, e.g. *tasarwala* "to put on *sarāwīlu* 'trousers or drawers'" from the Persian *šalwār.*

1.3.1. Form I of the quadriliteral:

One common Form I of the quadriliteral exists, namely:

1- Form I *faᶜlala,* e.g. *daḥraǧa* "to roll".

1.3.1.1. The forms that are coordinated by an augment to Form I faᶜlala:

There exist six common patterns that are coordinated by an augment to Form I *faᶜlala.* Lumsden, *A Grammar of the Arabic language* 149-150 presents seven, and the list can be made much longer.

1- *faᶜlala* with the two last radicals identical, e.g. *šamlala* "to gather ripe dates and also to be active or nimble".

2- *fawᶜala* with the infixed *w* after the 1st radical, e.g. *ḥawqala* meaning *lā ḥawla wa-lā quwwata ᵓilla bi-l-lāhi* "there is no power and no strength save in God". It is a combination of syllables in a frequently used expression. Other examples similar to *ḥawqala* in being a combination of syllables in well-known expressions, but which are formed according to *faᶜlala* and not to *fawᶜala,* are *basmala* "to say *bi-smi l-lāhi* "in the name of God", *ǧaᶜfada* "to say *ǧuᶜiltu fidāka* "may I become your ransom!", *ḥasbala* "to say *ḥasbī l-lāhu* "God is sufficient for me" and *ḥamdala* "to say *al-ḥamdu li-l-lāhi* "praise belongs to God".

3- *fay^c^ala* with the infixed *y* after the 1st radical, e.g. *bayṭara* "to practise the veterinary art or farriery".

4- *fa^c^wala* with the infixed *w* after the 2nd radical, e.g. *ǧahwara* "to utter one's speech in a loud voice".

5- *fa^c^nala* with the infixed *n* after the 2nd radical, e.g. *qalnasa* "to put on a cap called *qalansuwa"*. Abū Ḥanafī, *Maqṣūd* 2 reckons as well six forms that are coordinated by an augment to Form I of the quadriliteral only, but for the form *fay^c^ala,* he has the example *^c^aṯyara* "to stumble".

6- *fa^c^lā* with the suffixed *alif maqṣūra* after the 3rd radical, e.g. *qalsā* "to put on a cap called *qalansuwa".*

The following more uncommon forms can be added:

<u>*A- forms with prefix befiore the 1st radical:*</u>

7- the *t: taf^c^ala,* e.g. *tarmasa* "to absent oneself from battle" from *ramasa* "to conceal" (cf. Volck/Kellgren, *Ibn Mālik* 10, Suyūṭī, *Muzhir II,* 27, Howell, II-III, 255).

8- the *s: saf^{c}ala,* e.g. *sanbasa* "to hasten" from *nabasa* (cf. Suyūṭī, *Muzhir II,* 27, Volck/ Kellgren, *Ibn Mālik* 9, Howell, II-III, 255, Wright, II, 47).

9- the ^{c}*: ^{c}af^{c}ala,* e.g. *zahzaqa* "to laugh much" i.e. *ʾahzaqa* (cf. al-Ḫalīl in his introduction to the Kitāb al-^{c}ayn translated by Haywood, *Lexicography* 32, Volck/Kellgren, *Ibn Mālik* 9, Ibn Manẓūr, III, 1878, Howell, II-III, 254, Wright, II, 48).

10- the *h: haf^{c}ala,* e.g. *halqama* "to swallow" (cf. Suyūṭī, *Muzhir II,* 27, Howell, II-III, 255).

11- the *m: maf^{c}ala,* e.g. *marḥaba* "to welcome" (cf. Suyūṭī, *Muzhir II,* 27).

12- the *n: naf^{c}ala,* e.g. *narǧasa* "to be dirty" (cf. Suyūṭī, *Muzhir II,* 27).

13- the *y: yaf^{c}ala,* e.g. *yarnaʾa* "to dye red with henna" (cf. Suyūṭī, *Muzhir II,* 27).

B- forms with infix after the 1st radical:

14- The ^{c}*: fa^{c}lala,* e.g. *ṯa^{c}ǧara* "to shed blood or something else" (cf. Fleisch, *Traité II,* 441; for more examples concerning this particular form see 441-442).

15- the *m: famᶜala* (cf. Suyūṭī, Muzhir II, 27), e.g. *zamlaqa* "to eject (the stallion) its semen before insertion" (cf. Volck/Kellgren, *Ibn Mālik* 10, Howell, II-III, 255).

16- the *n: fanᶜala* (cf. Volck/Kellgren, *Ibn Mālik* 10, Suyūṭī, *Muzhir* II, 27, ᶜAbd al-Ḥamīd, *Taṣrīf* 599), e.g. *danqaᶜa l-rağulu* "the man became poor and clave to the earth" (cf. Ibn ᶜUṣfūr, I, 171, Howell, II-III, 257).

17- the *h: fahᶜala* (cf. Suyūṭī, *Muzhir II,* 27), e.g. *rahmasa* "to conceal" from *ramasa* (cf. Volck/Kellgren, *Ibn Mālik* 9, Howell, II-III, 255; for more examples concerning this particular form see Fleisch, *Traité II,* 440-441).

C- forms with infix after the 2nd radical:

18- the *ᵓ: faᶜᵓala,* e.g. *barᵓala l-dīku* "the cock ruffled the feathers of his neck" (cf. Howell, II-III, 257).

19- the *t: faᶜtala,* e.g. *kaltaba* "to act with slyness" (cf. Volck/Kellgren, *Ibn Mālik* 10, Howell, II-III, 255).

20- the *ᶜ: faᶜᶜala,* e.g. *ḫayᶜala* "to walk slowly because of a disturbance" (cf. Fleisch, *Traité II,* 442. For more examples concerning this particular form see 442-443).

21- the 1st radical: *faᶜfala,* e.g. *zahzaqa* in the meaning of *ᵓazhaqa* "to destroy" (cf. Suyūṭī, *Muzhir II,* 27). However, according to Ibn Manẓūr, III, 1878 and others already mentioned, *zahzaqa* is in the meaning of $^{\jmath}$*ahzaqa* "to laugh boisterously, which classifies it under ^{c}af^{c}ala mentioned above.

22- the *m: fa*^{c}*mala,* e.g. *ğalmaṭa* "to shave (one's head)" from *ğalaṭa* (cf. Howell, II-III, 255, Wright, II, 47).

23- the *y: fa*^{c}*yala* (cf. Suyūṭī, *Muzhir II,* 27, ^{c}Abd al-Ḥamīd, *Taṣrīf* 599), e.g. ^{c}*aḏyaṭa* "(a man) stooled in coition" (cf. Volck/Kellgren, *Ibn Mālik* 9, Howell, II-III, 255).

<u>*D- forms with suffix:*</u>

24- the *r: fa*^{c}*lara,* e.g. *šamḫara* "to be proud" from *šamaḫa* "to be high" (cf. Fleisch, *Traité II,* 444).

25- the *s: fa*^{c}*lasa,* e.g. *ḫalbasa* "to seduce and take away" from *ḫalaba* "to delude" (cf. Volck/Kellgren, *Ibn Mālik* 9, Suyūṭī, *Muzhir II,* 27, Howell, II-III, 254, Wright, II, 47, Fleisch, *Traité II,* 444).

26- the *l: fa*^{c}*lala,* e.g. *šam*^{c}*ala* "to spread itself" from *šama*^{c}*a* "to be scattered" (cf. Wright, II, 47, Fleisch, *Traité II,* 443).

27- the *m: fa*^{c}*lama,* e.g. ġalṣama "cut his epiglottis" from ġalaṣa (cf. Volck/Kellgren, *Ibn Mālik* 10, Suyūṭī, *Muzhir II,* 27,

Howell, II-III, 255; for more examples concerning this particular form see Fleisch, *Traité II,* 443-444).

28- the *n: faʿlana,* e.g. *qaṭrana* "to smear (the camel) with pitch" from *qaṭara* (cf. Suyūṭī, *Muzhir II,* 27, Volck/Kellgren, *Ibn Mālik* 9, Howell, II-III, 255, Wright, II, 48).

1.3.2. The derived forms of the quadriliteral:

Three derived forms are common. A 4th more anomalous form exists as well. They are the following:

1- Form II *tafaʿlala,* e.g. *tadaḥraǧa* "to roll along".

2- Form III *ʾifʿanlala,* e.g. *ʾiḥranǧama* "to gather together in a mass".

3- Form IV *ʾifʿalalla,* e.g *ʾiqšaʿarra* "to shudder with horror".

4- Form V *ʾifʿallala,* e.g. *ʾihrammaʿa* "to be fast in the race".

1.3.2.1. The forms that are coordinated by more than an augment to Form II tafaʿlala:

Five common patterns are coordinated to it.

1- *tafa^{c}lala* with the prefixed *t* and the two last radicals identical, e.g. *tağalbaba* "to put on a *ğilbābun*".

2- *tafaw^{c}ala* with the prefixed *t* and the infixed *w* after the 1st radical, e.g. *tağawraba* "to put on a *ğawrābun,* "a sock" from the root *ğ r b.*

3- *tafay^{c}ala* with the prefixed *t* and the infixed *y* after the 1st radical, e.g. *tašayṭana* "to act like a devil" from the root *š ṭ n.*

4- *tafa^{c}wala* with the prefixed *t* and the infixed *w* after the 2nd radical, e.g. *tarahwaka* "to show a feebleness in one's walk" from the root *r h k.*

5- *tamaf^{c}ala* with the prefixed *t* and the infixed *m* before the 1st radical, e.g. *tamaskana* "to become poor" from the root *s k n.*

The more uncommon forms that can be added are the following:

A- The following form with infix after the 1st radical:

6- the *h: tafah^{c}ala,* e.g. *tarahšafa* "to suck" from *rašafa* (cf. Volck/Kellgren, *Ibn Mālik* 9, Howell, II-III, 255).

B- The following forms with infix after the 2nd radical:

7- the *n: tafa^{c}nala,* e.g. *taqalnasa* "to put on oneself a cap" (cf. Ibn ^{c}Uṣfūr, I, 168, Suyūṭī, *Muzhir II,* 27).

8- the *y: tafa^{c}yala,* e.g. *tarahya^{c}a* "(the clouds) moved, and were prepared for the rain" (cf. Ibn Manẓūr, III, 1748, ^{c}Abd al-Ḥamīd, *Taṣrīf* 599).

C- The following forms with suffix:

9- the *t: tafa^{c}lata,* e.g. *ta^{c}afrata* "to act as a devil" (cf. Suyūṭī, *Muzhir II,* 27, Wright, II, 48).

10- the *l: tafa^{c}lala,* e.g. *tašama^{c}ala* "to disperse itself" from *šama^{c}a* (for discussions see Fleisch, *Traité II,* 443).

11- the *alif maqṣūra: tafa^{c}lā* (cf. Suyūṭī, *Muzhir II*, 27, ^{c}Abd al-Ḥamīd, *Taṣrīf* 599), e.g. *tasalqā* "to be thrown down upon one's back" from *salqā* (cf. Volck/Kellgren, *Ibn Mālik* 10, Howell, II-III, 255).

1.3.2.2. The forms that are coordinated by more than an augment to Form III ^{ɔ}if^{c}anlala:

Two common patterns are coordinated to it:

1- *ʾifʿanlasa* with the prefixation of the hamza, the infixation of the *n* after the 2nd radical and the suffixation of the *s,* e.g. *ʾiqʿansasa* "to have a hump in front" from the root *q ʿ s.*

2- *ʾifʿanlā* with the prefixation of the hamza, the infixation of the *n* after the 2nd radical and the suffixation of the alif maqṣūra, e.g. *ʾislanqā* "to lay on one's back" from the root *s l q.*

1.4. Form I verbal nouns of the triliteral

The *maṣdar* "verbal noun" is termed by Sībawaihi, I, 11 as *ʾism al-ḥadaṯ* "the noun of the action", or *ʾism al-ḥadaṯ wa-l-ḥadaṯāna* "the noun of both the action and the accident (of the agent)" (cf. Zamaḫšarī, 16).

Zamaḫšarī, 96-97 cites thirty-two forms among which some pertain to other forms than the strong verb, Wright, I, 111-112 mentions fourty-four, Howell, I, fasc. IV 1516-1517 mentions fourty-six forms and Ibn Mālik, *Lāmīya* verse 62-70 mentions fourty-nine forms.

<u>*A- The most common forms:*</u>

1- *faʿlun* e.g. *qatlun* "killing".

2- *fiʿlun* e.g. *fisqun* "profligacy".

3- *fu^c^lun* e.g. *šuġlun* "occupying".

4- *fa^c^latun* e.g. *raḥmatun* "having mercy".

5- *fi^c^latun* e.g. *nišdatun* "seeking".

6- *fu^c^latun* e.g. *kudratun* "being turbid".

7- *fa^c^lā* e.g. *da^c^wā* "praying".

8- *fi^c^lā* e.g. *ḏikrā* "remembering".

9- *fu^c^lā* e.g. *bušrā* "announcing happy news".

10- *fa^c^lānun* e.g. *layyānun* "softening".

11- *fi^c^lānu* e.g. *ḥirmānu* "refusing".

12- *fu^c^lānu* e.g. *ġufrānu* "forgiving".

13- *fa^c^alānu* e.g. *nazawānu* "escaping".

14- *fa^c^alun* e.g. *ṭalabun* "demanding".

15- fa^c^ilun e.g. *ḫaniqun* "strangling".

16- *fi^c^alun* e.g. *ṣiġarun* "being small".

17- *fu^c^lan* e.g. *hudan* "guiding".

18- *fa^c^alatun* e.g. *ġalabatun* "overcoming".

19- *fa^c^ilatun* e.g. *sariqatun* "stealing".

20- *faᶜālun* e.g. *ḏahābun* "going away".

21- *fiᶜālun* e.g. *ṣirāfun* "being in heat".

22- *fuᶜālun* e.g. *suʾālun* "requesting".

23- *faᶜālatun* e.g. *zahādatun* "abstinence".

24- *fiᶜālatun* e.g. *dirāyatun* "knowing".

25- *fuᶜūlun* e.g. *duḫūlun* "entering".

26- *faᶜūlun* e.g. *qabūlun* "accepting".

27- *faᶜīlun* e.g. *waǧīfun* "beating of the heart".

28- *fuᶜūlatun* e.g. *ṣuhūbatu*n "being reddish".

29- *mafᶜalun* e.g. *madḫalun* "entering".

30- *mafᶜilun* e.g. *marǧiᶜun* "retreating".

31- *mafᶜālun* e.g. *masᶜātun* "endeavouring".

32- *mafᶜilatun* e.g. *maḥmidatun* "praising".

<u>*B- The more uncommon forms:*</u>

33- *faᶜalūtun* e.g *ǧabarūtun* "being haughty".

34- *fuᶜalniyatun* e.g. *bulanhiyatun* "ease".

35- *tafʿalatun, tafʿilatun* or *tafʿulatun* e.g. *tahlakatun, tahlikatun* or *tahlukatun* "perishing".

36- *fuʿullatun* e.g. *ġulubbatun* “overcoming”.

37- *fuʿullā* (with final *alif maqṣūra)* e.g. *ġulubbā* (with final *alif maqṣūra).*

38- *fuʿlalun* e.g. *sūdadun* “being lord”.

39- *tufʿalun* e.g. *tudraʾun* “ability to repel foes”.

40- *fayʿalūlatun* e.g. *kaynanūnatun* “being”.

41- *faʿlūlatun* e.g. *ṣayrūratun* “becoming”.

42- *faʿīlatun* e.g. *šabībatun* “becoming adolescent.

43- *fāʿūlatun* e.g. *ḍārūratun* “affliction”.

44- *mafāʿilatun* e.g. *masāʾiyatun* “displeasing”.

1.4.1. Form I verbal nouns formed on the measure of the active participle:

Form I *maṣdar* can be formed on the measure of the active participle *fāʿilun.* An example of such a *maṣdar* is *qāʾiman* which is used instead of *qiyāman* in the phrase *qumtu qāʾiman* "I rose a rising" (cf. Wright, II, 132), in which it is a *maṣdar* formed according to the measure of the active participle *fā*ᶜ*ilun.* It occurs as well in the example *qum qā*ᵓ*iman* that is said instead of *qum qiyāman* in this verse cited by Ibn Fāris, *Ṣāḥibī* 237 who discusses the active participle as a substitute for the *maṣdar:*

> *"Qum qā*ᵓ*iman qum qā*ᵓ*iman*
> *laqīta* ᶜ*abdan nā*ᵓ*iman*
> "Get up! Get up!
> You met a sleeping slave!".

The active participle occurs also instead of the *maṣdar* in the following verse said by Bišr b.Abī Ḫāzim praising Aus b. Ḥāriṯa b. Laᵓm al-Ṭāᵓī, cited by Zamaḫšarī, 97, Ibn Yaᶜīš, VI, 51, Howell, I, fasc. IV, 1557, Fleischer, *Beiträge III,* 331, in which *kāfī* occurs anomalously in the nominative instead of the *kāfiyan,* the *y* being made vowelless by poetic licence, in the meaning of *kifāyatan:*

> *"kafā bi-l-na*ᵓ*yi min* ᵓ*asmā*ᵓ*a kāfī*
> *wa-laysa li-ḥubbihā* ᵓ*iḏ ṭāla šāfī".*
> "Sufficient indeed [for me as a trial] is the distance from Asmāᵓ;
> and there is no healer for the love of her, since it has lasted long".

Also, the *maṣdar* can occur on the measure of the active participle *fā*ᶜ*ilatun* (for a study see Ibn Fāris, *Ṣāḥibī* 237, Zamaḫšarī, 97, Ibn Yaᶜīš, VI, 50-52) as in the sur. 69: 8 *(fa-hal* *tarā lahum min bāqiyatin)* "Then seest thou any of them left surviving?", in which *bāqiyatin* has the meaning of *baqāʾin,* in the sur. 56: 2 *(laysa li-waqᶜatihā kāḏibatun)* "Then will no (soul) entertain falsehood", in which *kāḏibatun* has the meaning of *kaḏibun* and in the sur. 69: 4 *(fa-ʾammā ṯamūdu fa-ʾuhlikū bi-l-ṭāġiyati)* "But the Thamūd, - they were destroyed by a terrible storm of thunder and lightning!", in which *bi-l-ṭāġiyati* has the meaning of *bi-l-ṭuġyāni.*

1.4.2. Form I verbal nouns formed on the measure of the passive participle:

Form I *maṣdar* can be formed on the measure of the passive participle *mafᶜūlun.* An example of such a maṣdar is *al-maftūnu* that occurs instead of *al-fitnatu* in the sur. 68: 6 *(bi-ʾayyikumu l-maftūnu)* "Which of you is afflicted with madness" (cf. Ibn Fāris, *Ṣāḥibī* 237, Zamaḫšarī, 98 , Ibn Yaᶜīš, VII, 53, Åkesson, *Ibn Masᶜūd* 50: fol. 3b), in which it is a *maṣdar* formed according to the measure of the passive participle *mafᶜūlun.*

Also, the pattern of the *maṣdar* can occur instead of the pattern of the passive participle, and has its meaning (for some cases of the active and passive partiple occurring instead of the maṣdar and vice versa see Wright, II, 132-133), as in the sur. 31: 11 *(haḏā ḫalqu l-lāhi)* "Such is the Creation of God", in which *ḫalqu* occurs instead of *maḫlūqu* “the created"

1.4.3. Form I verbal nouns that denote intensity:

Some Form I *maṣdars* denote multiplication and intensification. The common ones are the following:

1- *tafᶜālun,* e.g. *tahdārun* "much fermentation" and *talᶜābun* "intensive sporting". The pattern *tifᶜālun* with the *t* given the kasra does not denote intensification, and the two examples that are known to be formed according to it are *tibyānun* "explanation" which occurs in the sur. 16: 89 *(wa-nazzalnā ᶜalayka l-kitāba tibyānan li-kulli šayʾin)* "And We have sent down to thee the Book explaining all things" and *tilqāʾun* "meeting" which occurs in the meaning of *laqyānun* "meeting" in a verse said by al-Rāʾī, cited by Howell, I, fasc. IV, 1561: *fa-l-yawma qaṣṣara ᶜan tilqāʾika l-ʾamalu* "For today hope has fallen short of meeting you".

2- *fiᶜᶜīlā* [with final *alif maqṣūra],* e.g. *al-ḥiṯṯīṯā* "much incitement (cf. Ibn Manẓūr, II, 773, Lane, I, 512) " and *al-dillīlā* "much guidance " (cf. Ibn Manẓūr, II, 1414, Lane, I, 901). Other examples are *qittītā* "much mischief-making", *hiǧǧīrā* "much evil-speaking" and *ḫillīfā* "being much engrossed with the business of the *Ḫilāfa"* (cf. Daqr, *Muᶜǧam 57).* The last example occurs in the saying said by ᶜUmar in the tradition *lawlā l-ḫillīfā la-ʾaḏḏantu* "Had I not been much engrossed with the buisness of the Ḫilāfa, I would chant the call to prayer".

1.5. The derived forms of the verbal nouns of the triliteral and Form I and the derived forms of the quadriliteral

The forms of the maṣdar of the derived forms of the triliteral and of Form I and the derived forms of the quadriliteral verb are divided between those that are analogous and those that are not analogous with their verbs.

1.5.1. The forms that are analogous with their verbs:

Many of the forms of the *maṣdar* of the derived forms of the triliteral and of Form I and the derived forms of the quadriliteral verb are analogous with their verbs. The reason of this resemblance in forms is according to Ibn Yaᶜīš, VI, 47, that these verbs' forms follow special measures and do not vary as the forms of Form I of the triliteral of which the vowel of the 2nd radical in many cases alternate in the perfect and in the imperfect.

Some of the forms of the *maṣdar* of the derived forms of the triliteral and of the quadriliteral that follow the specific forms of verbs, are presented in the following manner by Zamaḫšarī, 97:

> *"ᵓafᶜala ᵓifᶜālun, ᵓiftaᶜala ᵓiftiᶜālun, ᵓinfaᶜala ᵓinfiᶜālun, ᵓistafᶜala ᵓistifᶜālun, ᵓifᶜalla ᵓifᶜilālun, ᵓifᶜālla ᵓifᶜīlālun, ᵓifᶜawwala ᵓifᶜiwwālun, ᵓifᶜawᶜala ᵓifᶜīᶜālun, ᵓifᶜanlala ᶜifᶜinlālun, tafāᶜala tafāᶜulun* and *ᵓifᶜalalla ᵓifᶜillālun".*

A- The common forms of the derived forms of the masdar of the triliteral:

1- Form II: *tafᶜīlun, tafᶜilatun, tafᶜulatun, tafᶜālun, tifᶜālun fiᶜᶜālun, fiᶜᶜilayun* and *fiᶜᶜīlāʾu.*

2- Form III: *mufāᶜalatun, fiᶜālun, fīᶜālun* and *fiᶜᶜālun.*

3- Form IV: *ʾifᶜālun.*

4- Form V: *tafaᶜᶜulun* and *tifiᶜᶜālun.*

5- Form VI: *tafāᶜulun, tafāᶜalun* and *tafāᶜilun.*

6- Form VII: *ʾinfiᶜālun.*

7- Form VIII: *ʾiftiᶜālun* and *fiᶜᶜālun.*

8- Form IX: *ʾifᶜilālun.*

9- Form X: *ʾistifᶜālun.*

10- Form XI: *ʾifᶜīlālun.*

11- Form XII: *ʾifᶜīᶜālun.*

12- Form XIII: *ʾifᶜiwwālun.*

13- Form XIV: *ʾifᶜinlālun.*

14- Form XV: *ʾifᶜinlāʾun.*

B- The masdars of Form I of the quadriliteral and of the derived forms:

1- Form I: *fa^clalatun, fi^clālun* and *fa^clālun.*

2- Form II: *tafa^clulun.*

3- Form III: *^ɔif^cinlālun.*

4- Form IV: *^ɔif^cillālun.*

1.5.2. The forms that are not analogous with their verbs:

Some of the common forms are the following:

1- *fi^{cc}ālun,* e.g. *killāmun* "a talk", from Form II *kallama* "to talk to". The pattern occurs by the Yemenites (cf. Rabin, 37). Another example is *kiḏḏābun* which occurs in the sur. 78: 28 *(wa-kaḏḏabū bi-^ɔāyātinā kiḏḏāban)* "But they (impudently) treated our signs as false".

2- *fi^cālun* and *fī^cālun,* e.g. *qitālun* and *qītālun* "a fight, a battle" from Form III *qātala* "to fight against".

3- *tifi^{cc}ālun,* e.g. *tiḥimmālun* "a burden" from Form V *taḥammala* "to burden oneself". Another example that can be added is *timillāqun* "affection", which occurs in this verse said by an unknown poet, cited by Zamaḫšarī, 97, Ibn Ya^cīš, VI, 47,

IX, 157, Mulūkī 194, Howell, I, fasc. IV, 1538, Åkesson, Ibn Masᶜūd 107-108):

> *"Ṯalāṯatu ᵓaḥbābin fa-ḥubbun ᶜalāqatun*
> *wa-ḥubbun timillāqun wa-ḥubbun huwa l-qatlu".*
> "There are three loves; for there is a love that is attachment,
> and a love that is affection, and a love that is murder".

4 - *fiᶜlālun,* e.g. *zilzālun* "a concussion, convulsion, an earthquake" from Form I of the quadriliteral *zalzala* "to shake".

1.6. The perfect

The perfect verb, *al-māḍī*, is the verb that refers to an action that occurred in the past. It is *mabnī* "undeclinable" and takes suffixes which refer to the tense, number, gender and person.

*1.6a. binā*ᵓ *"undeclinability" and* ᵓ*i*ᶜ*rāb "declinablility":*

In the field of syntax, *binā*ᵓ "uninflectedness, undeclinability, invariability" (for definitions see de Sacy, I, 395, Lane, I, 260) implies that the word's ending is invariable whereas *i*ᶜ*rāb* "inflection, declension" suggests that the ending's state varies in accordance with the operator governing it (for discussions concerning both these terms see Bohas/Kouloughli, *Linguistic* 53-55).

*I*ᶜ*rāb* can as well refer to the formal *i*ᶜ*rāb,* which is the complete vowelling of the word (cf. ᶜUkbarī, *Masā*ᵓ*il* 102-105, Owens, *Foundations* 40). Thus the formal ᵓ*i*ᶜ*rāb* is different from the syntactical ᵓ*i*ᶜ*rāb,* as the latter is mainly concerned with the ending of the declinable word in accordance with its operator's rule (cf. Carter, *Linguistics [Širbīnī, Āğurrūmīya]* 37: 2. 15 (1)).

The question concerning which of the three parts of speech, the noun, verb or particle, is entitled to be declinable or undeclinable, has been a debated subject by many Arab grammarians (e.g. Zağğāğī, *Īḍāḥ* 77-82; for discussions see Versteegh, *Zağğāğī* 127-128). The declension has been given principally to the nouns whereas the undeclinability has been given to the verbs, - with the exception of the imperfect -, and to the particle.

1.6b. The undeclinability of the perfect:

The reason why the perfect is undeclinable and why its marker of undeclinability is a vowel, namely the fatḥa, is that the perfect is partly similar to the noun. Its vowelling separates it from the undeclinable imperative, which does not present any similarity with the noun, and which for this reason is given a marker that does not exist in the noun, namely the sukūn (for discussions see Ibn Yaᶜīš, VII, 4-5).

The following arguments are introduced concerning the reasons of its undeclinability:

1- Like the noun it can function as a modifier, *ṣifah,* to the indefinite noun. This is remarked in the sentence *maratu bi-rağulin ḍaraba wa-ḍāribin* "I passed by a man who hit and who was hitting", in which both the perfect *ḍaraba* and the active participle of the noun *ḍāribin* have the same function (cf. ibid 4).

2- In the same manner as the active participle, it can function as a *ḫabar* "predicate" in a nominal sentence. An example is *zaydun qāma* "Zaid was getting up", in which the perfect *qāma* is a predicate to the topic Zaydun in the same manner as the active participle *qāʾimun* is a predicate to the same topic in the sentence *Zaydun qāʾimun.*

3- It can as well have the same meaning as the imperfect, which is considered to be the form that is similar to the declinable noun, and thus can replace it. For instance in a sentence as *ʾin qumta qumtu* "If you rise, I shall rise", the perfects *qumta qumtu* that occur after the conditional *ʾin* can be used instead of the imperfect forms *taqum ʾaqum* after the same conditional, i.e. *ʾin taqum ʾaqum.*

4- A resemblance that exists between the perfect and the active participle form of the noun, is that the active participle refers to past time when it is used as the first element of an *ʾiḍāfa* construction, as in e.g. *ʾanā qātilu ġulāmika* "I am the killer of your servant", in which the active participle *qātilu* that is put in the nominative before the noun in the genitive *ġulāmika,* shows that the action of the killing is completed, in the same manner as *qataltu* does in the sentence *ʾanā qataltu ġulāmaka* "I have killed your servant". The difference between the perfect and the active participle is that the active participle that occurs as a first element of an *ʾiḍāfa* construction, and thus refers to a completed action in the past, is unable to govern the noun after it in the accusative as the perfect does, so *ʾanā qātilu ġulāmika* is said for this meaning and not *ʾanā qātilu ġulāmaka* (cf. Suyūṭī, *Ašbāh III,* 535-536).

According to the theory of Ibn Yaʿīš, VII, 5, the reason why the perfect's ending is given a fatḥa and not a ḍamma, is that some Arabs used the ḍamma instead of the *ū* to mark the pl., e.g. *qāmu* said instead of *qāmū* "they rose /masc. pl.". Another example is *kānu* said instead of *kānū* in the following verse said by an anonymous poet, cited by Muʾaddib, *Taṣrīf* 15, Ibn Yaʿīš, VII, 5, Ibn Ḫālawaihi, *Qirāʾāt* I, 352, Ibn al-Anbārī, *Inṣāf* Q. 72, 222 and Howell, I, fasc. II, 517 with *wa-law* instead of *fa-law:*

> *"Fa-law ʾanna l-ʾaṭibbāʾī kānū ḥawlī*
> *wa-kāna maʿa l-ʾaṭibbāʾI l-ʾusātu"*
> "O, if the physicians had been around me
> and the surgeons were with the physicians!"

Other examples with the ḍamma replacing the suffixed pronoun of the nominative, the *ū,* presented by Muʾaddib, *Taṣrīf* 296 are *lam yaḏhabu ʾiḫwatuka* "your brothers did not go" said by some Arabs with *lam yaḏhabu* instead of *lam yaḏhabū.* Some read as well the sur. 53: 31 as *(li-yağziya l-laḏīna ʾasāʾu)*

"So that He rewards those who do Evil" with *ʾasāʾu* instead of *ʾasāʾū*.

1.6.1. The forms of the perfect:

The forms of the perfect *faᶜala* are the following:

	sing.	dual	pl.
1st	*faᶜal-tu*		*faᶜal-n(a)ā*
2nd masc.	*faᶜal-ta*	*faᶜal-tum(a)-ā*	*faᶜal-tum*
2nd fem.	*faᶜal-ti*	*faᶜal-tum(a)-ā*	*faᶜal-tunna*
3rd masc.	*faᶜala*	*faᶜal(a)-ā*	*faᶜal(u)-ū [+ ā]*
3rd fem.	*faᶜala-t*	*faᶜal(a)-t(a)ā*	*faᶜal-na*

1.6.1.1. Some remarks concerning the perfect's forms:

The forms that are taken up at first are those in which the perfect's 3rd radical is vowelled. This vowel can be a fatḥa or a ḍamma. The forms of which the 3rd radical is vowelless are presented afterwards.

1.6.1.1.1. The perfect's 3rd radical is vowelled by a fatḥa:

The fatḥa vowels the 3rd radical in the 3rd person of the masc. sing. *faᶜala*, the 3rd person of the fem. sing. *faᶜala-t* and the 3rd person of the masc. dual *faᶜal(a)-ā* and fem. dual *faᶜal(a)-t(a)ā.*

<u>1- *faᶜala*</u>

As stated previously, the perfect's marker of undeclinability is a fatḥa.

<u>2- *faᶜala-t:*</u>

The vowelless suffix *-t* in the 3rd person of the fem. sing. *faᶜala-t* marks the fem. and is not a pronoun. It can be compared to the vowelled suffix *-t* of the 1st and 2nd persons of the sing., namely the *-tu* in *faᶜal-tu* "I did", the *-ta* in *faᶜal-ta* "/2 masc. sing." and the *-ti* in *faᶜal-ti* "/2 fem. sing.".

The proof of it being a marker of the feminine is that if it had been a pronoun it would have been elided by the manifested agent that can follow it (cf. Åkesson, *Ibn Masᶜūd* 64: fol. 9a) as it is impossible to combine two agents for the same verb. As an example *ḍaraba-t Hindun* "Hind hit" can be mentioned, in which the *-t* marker of the fem. in *ḍaraba-t* is not elided by the agent following it, i.e. *Hindun*, as *ḍaraba Hindun* is not accepted. No agent pronoun is suffixed to this form of the fem. as the *-t* suffix is a marker of the fem., and alike the 3rd person of the masc. sing. *faᶜala,* the agent is considered as latent (cf. Versteegh, *Language* 81).

It can be remarked that the elision of the agent pronoun is by contrast carried out when the perfect's form of the 3rd person of the masc. pl. is combined with a separated agent following it, as it looses its *-ū* agent suffix to hinder the combination of two agents, e.g. *ḍaraba l-awlādu* is said instead of *ḍarabū l-ᵓawlādu* "the children hit".

3- *faᶜal(a)-ā:*

There exists a similarity between the suffix *-ā* of the dual of the 3rd person of the masc. *faᶜal(a)-ā* and the suffix *-ā* of the dual of the 3rd person of the masc. of the independent pronoun of the nominative of the 3rd person of the masc. sing. *hum(a)-ā* "they both /dual".

4- *faᶜala-t(a)ā:*

The infix *-t* marker of the fem. sing. in the 3rd person of the dual of the fem. pl. *faᶜala-t(a)ā* is underlyingly vowelless alike the suffix *-t* in the 3rd person of the fem. sing. *fa^cala-t.* It is however given a fatḥa to hinder the combination of two vowelless segments, as it precedes the vowelless *ā.* Hence *faᶜala-t(a)ā* is said and not *faᶜala-t-ā.*

It can be noted that the suffix *-ā* of the dual of the 3rd person of the fem. sing. in *faᶜala-t(a)ā* is the same as the one in the 3rd person of the masc. sing. *faᶜal(a)-ā.*

1.6.1.1.2. The perfect's 3rd radical is vowelled by a ḍamma:

The ḍamma vowels the 3rd radical in the 3rd person of the masc. pl. *faᶜal(u)-ū.*

1- *faᶜal(u)-ū [+ alif mamdūda]:*

The ḍamma vowels generally the 3rd radical in the 3rd person of the masc. pl. *faᶜal(u)-ū [+ alif mamdūda]* "they did /masc. pl.". Concerning the suffix *-ū [+ alif mamdūda]* in *faᶜal(u)-ū [+ alif mamdūda],* we observe that it is the same as the *-ū* suffix of the base form of the pronoun of the nominative of the 3rd person of the masc. pl. *hum(u)-ū [+ alif mamdūda]* "they /masc. pl.".

The rule of having a ḍamma preceding the *-ū* suffix *[+ alif mamdūda]* is not followed when it concerns a verb with 3rd weak radical of the conjugation *fa*ᶜ*ala* of which the 3rd weak radical is elided, e.g. *rama-w [+ alif mamdūda]* "they threw /masc. pl.".

The *alif mamdūda* suffixed after the *ū* of the pl. is termed as *alif al-wiqāya* "the guarding alif" (cf. Wright, I, 11). There exist different opinions concerning its occurrence.

According to al-Farrāᵓ's theory, this alif is suffixed after the *-ū* of the pl., so that it is possible to differentiate between the *ū* which is a radical in verbs with 3rd weak radical and the *ū* marking the pl. As an example of a verb in the sing. ending with a *w* radical, we can mention *yad*ᶜ*ū* "he calls" and as an example of a verb in the jussive ending with the suffixed pronoun of the nominative of the masc. pl., the *ū,* preceding the *alif mamdūda,* we can mention *lam yad*ᶜ*ū* "they did not call". Had it not been for the *alif madmdūda,* then both the singular and the pl. would be mixed together.

Some Arabs use defectively the indicative mood of the sing. in some cases of weak 3rd radical verbs instead of the correct jussive mood (for a study of such cases see Zamaḫšarī, 184-185, Ibn Yaᶜīš, X, 104-107, Wright, IV 389) by maintaining the 3rd weak radical instead of eliding it. An example is *lam yad*ᶜ*ū* "he did not call" with the maintainance of the *ū* said instead of the correct *lam yad*ᶜ*u* (cf. Ibn Masᶜūd, fol. 5a) with its elision. Had it not been for the *alif mamdūda* after the *ū,* then both the sing., i.e. *lam yadᶜū* "he did not call" in this defective dialectal variant, and the pl., i.e. *lam yadᶜū* (with the *alif mamdūda* after the *ū)* "they did not call" would have been mixed up together.

This defective maintainace of the *ū* in the jussive occurs in this verse said by an unknown poet, cited by Zamaḫšarī, 184, Ibn Yaᶜīš, X, 104, Howell, IV, fasc. I, 1576 and Wright, IV 389, in which *lam tahǧū* occurs instead of *lam tahǧu:*

> *"Haǧawta Zabbāna ṯumma ǧiᵓta muᶜtaḏiran*
> *min haǧwi Zabbāna lam tahǧū wa-lam tadaᶜi".*
> "You did satirize Zabbān: then you came, apologizing for satirizing Zabbān: you did not satirize [him], nor did you leave [him] alone".

According to the theory of al-Aḫfaš, the alif is suffixed so that the wāw of the pl. is not mixed up with the wāw of the conjunction (cf. ᶜAbd al-Tawwāb‘s note on Rāzī, in Ḫalīl b. Aḥmad ..., *Ḥurūf* 135). An example is the phrase *ḥḍrwtkllm* (cf. Åkesson, *Ibn Masᶜūd* 54: fol. 5a) written without diatritic signs and without an alif after the *w*. It can be read in two manners: *ḥaḍara wa-takallama* "He came and talked" or *ḥaḍarū takallama* "they came, he talked" causing an inevitable confusion, which is why the presence or the absence of the alif after the *w* is significant.

1.6.1.1.3. The perfect's 3rd radical is vowelless:

The 3rd radical of the perfect's basic form *fa^c^al-* is given a sukūn when the vowelled agent suffixes, the *-t:* i.e. *tu, ta* and *ti,* and the *-n:* i.e. *na,* are attached to it.

These forms are: *fa^c^al-tu* "I did", *fa^c^al-ta* "/2 masc. sing.", *fa^c^al-ti* "/2 fem. sing.", *fa^c^al-tum(a)ā, fa^c^al-tum, fa^c^al-tunna, fa^c^al-n(a)ā* "/1 pl." and *fa^c^al-na* "/3rd fem. pl.".

The reason of the vowellness of the 3rd radical is to hinder the forbidden combination of four consecutive vowels (for this principle see Zağğāğī, *Īḍāḥ* 75, Ḥassān, *Uṣūl* 228). Hence *fa^c^al-tu, fa^c^al-ta, fa^c^al-ti, fa^c^al-nā and fa^c^al-na* are said and not *fa^c^ala-tu, fa^c^ala-ta, fa^c^ala-ti, fa^c^ala-nā* and *fa^c^ala-na.*

The perfect's 3rd radical is not vowelless when the pronoun of the accusative is suffixed to it, e.g. *ḍaraba-ka* "he hit you /masc. sing." which is said with the succession of the four vowels, and not *ḍarab-ka.* The reason why the Arab grammarians accept the succession of the four vowels in *ḍaraba-ka* is that they consider the suffixed pronoun of the agent as one with its verb, whereas they consider the suffixed pronoun of the object as another word separated from it, thus leading to a proper rule as the acceptance of the succession of the four vowels. The verb is in need of an agent, manifest or suppressed, which is why the verb is considered as one with its pronoun of the agent, whereas it can manage without an object, which is the reason why it and its pronoun of the object are considered as two separate words (cf. Ibn Ǧinnī, *Sirr I,* 221).

1- *faᶜal-n(a)ā:*

There exists a similarity between the *-n* infix in the perfect's form of the 1st person of the pl. *faᶜal-n(a)ā* "we did" and the first consonant *n* of the independent pronoun of the agent of the 1st person of the pl. *naḥnu* "we" (cf. Åkesson, *Ibn Masᶜūd* 58: fol. 6b). The *-ā* ending in it is formed according to the ending in the independent pronoun of the 1st person of the pl. *ᵓinnanā* "we" and is, on the other hand, necessary to differenciate it from the *-na* that marks the 3rd person of the fem. pl. in the perfect form *faᶜal-na* "they did /fem. pl.".

2- *faᶜal-tum(a)-ā:*

The perfect's forms of the duals of the 2nd person of the masc. and of the fem. sing. *faᶜal-tum(a)-ā* "you did /masc. or fem. dual" are common.

The *-m* infix is added to the perfect's form before the dual *-ā* suffix so that there is no confusion between the pronoun's ending *-tum(a)ā* of the 2nd person of the dual and the pronoun's ending *-t(a)ā* of the 2nd person of the masc. sing. to which the alif of saturation can in some cases, as in poetry and in pause, be suffixed to (cf. Åkesson, *Ibn Mas^cūd* 56-58: fol. 5b). In other words the *-m* infix is added to avoid confusing the alif of the dual with the alif of saturation (cf. Ibn al-Anbārī, *Inṣāf* Q. 96, 284).

An example that can be taken up with the alif of saturation suffixed to the pronoun of 2nd person of the masc. sing. is *ᵓant(a)ā* said instead of *ᵓanta,* which occurs in the following verse cited by ibid, Q. 96, 284, Åkesson, *Ibn Masᶜūd* 56: fol. 5b):

> *"ᵓAḫūka ᵓaḫū mukāšaratin wa-ḍiḥkin*
> *wa-ḥayyāka l-ᵓālihu fa-kayfa ᵓantā?".*
> "Your brother is one who cleaves to cheerfulness and laughter
> And may God preserve your life, in which condition are you in?".

Another example occurs in this verse said by Sālim b. Dāra, cited by Muᵓaddib, *Taṣrīf* 25, Ibn al-Anbārī, *Inṣāf* Q. 45, 144, Q. 96, 284, Åkesson, *Ibn Masᶜūd* 148: (60):

> *"Yā Murra yā bna Wāqiᶜin yā ᵓantā*
> *ᵓanta l-laḏī ṭallaqta ᶜāma ǧuᶜtā".*
> "O Murr, O Ibn Wāqiᶜ, O you!
> It is you who divorced [your wife] in a year when you were hungry!".

The pronoun's ending *-tum(a)-ā* in the perfect's form *fa^cal-tum(a)-ā* is the same as the ending of the independent pronoun of the masc. and fem. of the dual *ᵓantum(a)-ā* (cf. Åkesson, *Ibn Masᶜūd* 56: fol. 5b). There exists as well a similarity between the dual ending *-m(a)-ā* in *ᵓantum(a)-ā* "you both" and the ending *-m(a)ā* of the independent pronoun of the 3rd person of the dual *hum(a)ā* "they both" (cf. ibid, 56-58: fol. 5b-6a).

3- *faᶜal-tum:*

The *-tum* ending in the perfect's of the 2nd person of the masc. pl. *faᶜal-tum* is formed according to the ending *-tum(a)ā* in the perfect's form of the 2nd person of the masc. pl. *faᶜal-tum(a)ā.* The *-tum* ending is underlyingly *-tum(u)ū* (+ alif mamdūda), and hence *faᶜal-tum* is underlyingly *faᶜal-tum(u)ū* [+ *alif mamdūda].*

The *-ū* suffix following the infix *-tum* is elided because of the dislike that the Arabs have for pronouns or nouns ending with an *-ū* preceded by a ḍamma, which they deem as a heavy combination. It can be remarked that the *-ū* suffix of the perfect's form of the 3rd person of the masc. pl. *faᶜal(u)ū* is not elided as it is not attached to a pronoun infix, but follows immediately the 3rd radical (cf. ibid, 58: fol. 6a).

Hence the only pronoun which exists in the language with a w preceded by a ḍamma is *huwa* "he" (cf. ibid). In the light of this principle that nouns cannot end with a *w* preceded by a ḍamma in nouns, the formation of the pl. of the noun *dalwun* "bucket" is *ʾadlin* and not *ʾadluwun* (cf. Ibn Ǧinnī, *de Flexione* 43, Zamaḫšarī, 185, Ibn Yaᶜīš, X, 107-108, Ibn Mālik, *Alfīya* 147, Goguyer's commentary to verse 617, Lane, I, 909, Wright, II, 209).

The verbs however can end with a *w* preceded by a ḍamma (cf. Ibn Ǧinnī, *de Flexione* 42-43, Ibn Yaᶜīš, X, 104) without that this combination is deemed as heavy, e.g. the imperfect's form of the 3rd person of the sing. *yaġz(u)ū* "he assaults" underlyingly *yaġz(u)w* and *yadᶜ(u)ū* "he calls" underlyingly *yadᶜ(u)w* before that the assimilation of the *w* to the *u* is carried out resulting in the lengthened *ū*.

The *-ū* suffix of the base form *faᶜal-tum(u)ū,* which is elided resulting in *faᶜal-tum*, is however maintained when a pronoun of the accusative is attached to the verb, because the *-ū* is not longer at the extremity of the word. An example is *ḍarab-tumū-hu* "you hit him /masc. pl." with the *-hu* object pronoun suffixed to it. Furthermore the pronoun of the accusative is also a reason why the verb is brought back to its base form (cf. Ibn Yaᶜīš, III, 95), as by principle the pronouns bring back the words to their base form (cf. Sībawaihi, I, 341-342).

4- *fa*^{c}*al-tunna:*

The *-na* suffix in the ending *-tunna* of the perfect's form of the 2nd person of the fem. pl. *fa*^{c}*al-tunna* is doubled differently from the *-na* suffix in the perfect's form of the 3rd person of the fem. pl. *fa*^{c}*al-na.*

According to a theory presented by Ibn Mas^{c}ūd (cf. Åkesson, *Ibn Mas*^{c}*ūd* 58: fol. 6b), its base form is *ḍarab-tum-na* with the *-na* marker of the fem. pl. following the suffixed pronoun of the 2nd person of the masc. pl. *-tum.* Then the *m* was assimilated to the *n* because of the proximity of the *m* to the *n* in the point of utterance, as the *m* originates between the lips and the *n* from the upper part of the nose. This interchange of the *m* for the *n* and vice versa is remarked for instance in ^{c}*anbarun* that becomes ^{c}*ambarun.*

According to another theory, the reason why the *n* is doubled in the ending *-tunna* of the 2nd person of the fem. pl. is that two nūns should arise as compared in number to the *m* and the *ū* in the ending *-tum(u)ū* of the 2nd person of the masc. pl. *fa*^{c}*al-tum(u)ū* (cf. Ibn Ya^{c}īš, III, 87, Howell, I, fasc. II, 516).

5- *fa*^{c}*al-na:*

There exists a similarity between the suffix *-na* in the the 3rd person of the fem. pl. of the perfect *fa*^{c}*al-na* and the suffix *-na* of the independent pronoun of the nominative (cf. Åkesson, *Ibn Mas^c^ūd* 54: fol. 5a) of the 3rd person of the fem. pl. *hun-na* "they /fem. pl.".

1.7. The imperfect

The imperfect verb, *al-muḍāri^{c}* refers to an action that can be incomplete, is still going on, or is carried out in the present, past or future time. It is declinable for mode and takes prefixes and in some cases as well infixes and suffixes which refer to the agent.

1.7a. The declinability of the imperfect:

The imperfect is declinable and vowelled by a ḍamma as its marker of declinability due to its resemblance to the active participle which pertains to the noun category and which is declinable (cf. Ibn Ya^{c}īš, VII, 6, Åkesson, *Ibn Mas^{c}ūd* 66: fol. 9b, Owens, *Foundations* 207-208).

So generally stated, the reason why the imperfect is declinable is its resemblance to the active participle form of the noun, which is a noun.

These are the principal arguments:

1- The phonological form of the imperfect *yaḍribu* and the active participle *ḍ(a)āribun* are commensurable regarding the vowelling or the vowellessness of both these forms' respective consonants (cf. Owens, *Foundations* 208).

2- Just like the active participle, the imperfect can occur as a modifier, *ṣifat,* of an indefinite noun. In a sentence as *hāḏā rağulun yaḍribu* "this is a hitting man", the imperfect that follows the indefinite noun functions as a modifier, and corresponds in its meaning to the modifier in the example *hāḏā rağulun ḍāribun* (cf. ibid).

3- The inceptive *la-* which is specific to be prefixed to nouns which it emphasizes, e.g. *ʾinna Zaydan la-qāʾimun* "verily Zaid is getting up", can be prefixed to the imperfect, i.e. *ʾinna Zaydan la-yaqūmu,* and the meaning is the same. This particular *la* cannot be made to precede the perfect, i.e. *ʾinna Zaydan la-qāma* with the very same specific meaning that this affirmative la- introduces.

4- The imperfect can be general, by which it is meant that it is vague, because it can be valid for the tenses of the present and future (cf. Ibn Ḫālawaihi, *Iʿrāb* 4), e.g. *yaḍribu* can mean "he hits, he is hitting or he shall hit". It is this vagueness that is considered as similar to the vagueness of the indefinite noun, e.g. *raʾaytu rağulan* "I saw a man", in which *rağulan* "a man" refers to an indefinite man.

5- The prefixation of the *s* or *sawfa* to the imperfect specifies its meaning by making it refer to a special tense which is the future, e.g. *Zaydun sa-yaḍribu* and *sawfa yaḍribu* "Zaid will hit", in the same manner as the prefixation of the definite article *l-* to the indefinite noun renders it definite, e.g. *raʾaytu l-rağula* "I saw the man".

6- The imperfect functions as a *ḥāl* "denotative of state", in e.g. *Zaydun yaḍribu,* and corresponds in its function and meaning to the active participle, in e.g. *Zaydun ḍāribun* "Zaid is hitting".

7- The dual and pl. suffixes. respectively *-āni* and *-ūna* of the imperfect and noun are similar (for a detailed discussion see Maḫzūmī, *Naḥw* 136-137).

8- The declension of the imperfect is specified with *al-rafᶜ* "the indicative mood" that corresponds to the nominative case of the nouns, *al-naṣb* "the subjunctive mood" that corresponds to the accusative case of the nouns and *al-ğazm* "the jussive mood" that corresponds to *al-ğarr* "the genitive case" of the nouns.

The question of the declinability of the imperfect has been discussed by the Kufans and Basrans (cf. Zağğāğī, *Iḍāḥ* 80-82, Ibn al-Anbārī, *Inṣāf* Q. 73, 224-225, ᶜUkbarī, *Masāʾil* 83-85, Ibn Yaᶜīš, VII, 12-14). The opinion of the Kufans concerning its declinability differs slightly from the Basrans. They agreed with the Basrans that the imperfect should be declinable, but believed that its declinability is original. By introducing this idea, they opposed the rule that the declinability is principal for the nouns, and assumed that it can as well apply to the verbs as in the case of the imperfect. Their main argument is that the imperfect could refer to different tenses, as the future or a continuous time in the sentences. As well as the use of the three moods, the indicative, subjunctive or jussive, imposes on it different significations. This flexibility similar to the noun's flexibility is according to them the reason of its original declinability.

1.7.1. The forms of the imperfect:

The forms of the imperfect *yafʿalu* are the following:

The forms of the perfect *faʿala* are the following:

	sing.	dual	pl.
1st	*ʾafʿalu*		*nafʿalu*
2nd masc.	*tafʿalu*	*tafʿal(a)-āni*	*tafʿal(u)-ūna*
2nd fem.	*tafʿal(i)-īna*	*tafʿal(a)-āni*	*tafʿal-na*
3rd masc.	*yafʿalu*	*yafʿal(a)-āni*	*yafʿal(u)-ūna*
3rd fem.	*tafʿalu*	*tafʿal(a)-āni*	*yafʿal-na*

1.7.1.1. Some remarks concerning the imperfect's forms:

The imperfect takes prefixes and in some cases infixes and suffixes which refer to the agent. The four prefixes of the imperfect are: the vowelled hamza, *t*, *y* and *n*. These segments can be combined in different mnemonic words, e.g. *ʾanaytu* or *naʾtī*.

The forms that are discussed at first are those with the imperfect prefixes vowelled by a fatḥa. Among them the forms with infixes and suffixes are taken up. Then the forms with the imperfect prefixes vowelled by a ḍamma in the derived forms and with a kasra in the dialectal variant *al-taltala* are discussed.

1.7.1.1.1. The forms with the imperfect prefixes vowelled by a fatḥa:

The imperfect prefixes are vowelled by a fatḥa in Form I of the active voice *ʾafʿalu, tafʿalu, yafʿalu* and *nafʿalu* on account of the lightness of the fatḥa, and also in the forms constituted of five segments or more in order to alleviate (cf. Åkesson, *Ibn Masʿūd* 68: fol. 10b). The forms that are constituted of five segments or more are the derived forms of the triliteral, namely Form V *ya-tafaʿʿalu,* Form VI *ya-tafāʿalu,* Form VII *ya-nfaʿilu,* Form VIII *yaftaʿilu,* Form IX *yafʿallu,* Form X *ya-stafʿilu* etc., and the derived forms of the quadriliteral, namely

Form II *ya-tafa*ᶜ*lalu,* Form III *yaf*ᶜ*anlilu,* Form IV *yaf*ᶜ*alillu and* Form V *yaf*ᶜ*allilu.*

An anomaly that can be mentioned in which the imperfect prefix is vowelled by a ḍamma, and not by a fatḥa, is *yu-harīqu* "to spill" from ᵓ*ahraqa,* that seems to be formed of five segments. It is basically Form IV *yu-rīqu* from ᵓ*arwaqa,* in which the *h* is anomalously infixed as a reaction to the phonological change that its middle weak radical has been subjected to (cf. Ibn Ǧinnī, *Sirr I,* 201).

1- ᵓ*af*ᶜ*alu:*

An agreement can be noted betwen the ᵓ*a* that is chosen as an imperfect prefix for the 1st person of the sing. ᵓ*af*ᶜ*alu* "I do" and the ᵓa prefix of the independent pronoun of the 1st person of the sing. ᵓ*anā* "I" (cf. Åkesson, *Ibn Mas*ᶜ*ūd* 66: fol. 10a).

2- *taf*ᶜ*alu:*

The form *taf*ᶜ*alu* is common for both the 2nd person of the masc. sing. and the 3rd person of the fem. sing.

An agreement can be noted betwen the *ta-* that is chosen as an imperfect prefix for the 2nd person of the masc. sing. *taf*ᶜ*alu* "you do" and the *-ta* suffix of the independent pronoun of the 2nd person of the masc. sing. *ʾan-ta.*

Furthermore the *t-* of the 3rd person of the fem. sing. *tafᶜalu* "she does" and the *-t* suffix of the perfect form *faᶜala-t* "she did" is the same (cf. Wright, *Comparative Grammar* 184). However differently from the voweless *-t* suffix of the perfect *faᶜala-t,* the *t-* prefix of the imperfect is given a vowel because by principle it is impossible to begin the word with a vowelless segment (cf. Åkesson, *Ibn Masᶜūd* 68: fol. 11a).

3- *yafᶜal-na:*

The *ya-* prefix is chosen for the 3rd person of the fem. pl. *yafᶜal-na* and not the *ta-* prefix as in its singular form *tafᶜalu,* to avoid the combination of two markers of the fem., i.e. the *-ta* prefix and the *-na* suffix, which is deemed as heavy in the same verb (cf. ibid, 70: fol. 11b).

4- *tafᶜal(i)-īna, tafᶜal(u)-ūna, yafᶜal(u)-ūna, tafᶜal(a)-āni, yafᶜal(a)-āni:*

a- The -ī infix in tafᶜal(i)-īna and the -ū infix in tafᶜal(u)-ūna and yafᶜal(u)-ūna:

The *-ī* infix in *tafᶜal(i)-īna* "you do /fem. sing." is the agent pronoun of the 2nd person of the fem. sing. according to the majority of the grammarians with the exception of al-Aḫfaš (cf. ibid, 62: fol. 8b). It detains the same position as an agent, alike the *-ū* infix which is the agent pronoun of the 2nd person of the masc. pl. in *tafᶜal(u)-ūna* "you do / masc. pl." and of the 3rd person of the masc. pl. in *yafᶜal(u)-ūna* "they do /masc. pl.". Al-Aḫfaš prefers to consider the *-ī* infix as a marker of feminization and regards the form *tafᶜal(i)-īna* as having a latent pronoun. His theory is based on the fact that both the 2nd person of the masc. and the 3rd person of the fem. sing. of the imperfect *tafᶜalu* are common and lack a prominent pronoun. It is on this basis and for the sake of analogy that al-Aḫfaš insisted in having the sings. of the imperfect as treated uniformly (cf. Howell, I, fasc. II, 519).

The choice of the *-ī* infix in this form that is specific for the fem. is justified by Ibn Masᶜūd (Åkesson, *Ibn Masᶜūd* 62: fol. 8b) who compares it with the *-ī* that replaces the *-hi* that marks the fem. sing. in the demonstratif pronoun *hāḏihi* which becomes *hāḏ(i)ī* in the expression *hāḏī ᵓamatu l-lāhi* "this is God's maid-servant" (for this substitution see Rāzī, in Ḫalīl b. Aḥmad ..., *Ḥurūf* 154, *Sībawaihi,* II, 341, Ibn Ǧinnī, *Sirr II,* 556, Zamaḫšarī, 176). This implies a closeness between the *hi* and the *ī* in marking the feminization and makes the *-ī* fit to be a marker of the fem. Furthermore, the *-ī* infix is necessary so that the sing. form *tafᶜal(i)-īna* would be distinguished from the pl. form of the fem. *tafᶜal-na* "you do /fem. pl." (cf. Åkesson, *Ibn Masᶜūd* 62: fol. 8b).

b- The -na suffix in taf^{c}al(i)-īna, taf^{c}al(u)-ūna, yaf^{c}al(u)-ūna, and the -ni suffix in taf^{c}al(a)-āni, yaf^{c}al(a)-āni:

The *-na* suffix in the endings *-īna* of the imperfect's form of the 2nd person of the fem. sing. *taf^{c}al(i)-īna* and *-ūna* of the 2nd and 3rd person of the masc. pl. *taf^{c}al(u)-ūna* and *yaf^{c}al(u)-ūna* respectively, is the marker of the indicative. It is elided in the jussive and subjunctive mood. It is different from the *-na* suffix attached to the 2nd and 3rd person of the fem. pl. *taf^{c}al-na* "you do /fem. pl." and *yaf^{c}al-na* "they do /fem. pl.", which in these forms is the marker of the fem. pl. alike the *-na* suffix in the 3rd person of the fem. pl. of the perfect *fa^{c}al-na* "they did /fem. pl.".

The *-ni* suffix in the ending *-āni* in the dual forms of the 2nd and 3rd persons *taf^{c}al(a)-āni* and *yaf^{c}al(a)-āni* respectively is also the marker of the indicative.

c- The -ā infix in the ending -āni in taf^{c}al(a)-āni and yaf^{c}al(a)-āni:

The *-ā* infix of the ending -āni in the dual forms of the 2nd and 3rd persons *taf^{c}al(a)-āni* and *yaf^{c}al(a)-āni* respectively, is the agent pronoun alike the suffix *-ā* of the dual of the perfect of the same persons, namely *fa^{c}al-tum(a)-ā* and *fa^{c}al(a)-ā* respectively.

The ending *-āni* in these forms is the same as the ending *-āni* of the dual in the noun, e.g. *ḍārib(a)-āni* "hitting /masc. dual". However, differently from the noun in which this ending marks the case of the nominative, and varies to the ending *-ayni* in the cases of the accusative and genitive, namely *ḍāriba-yni,* the ending *-āni* in the imperfect does not vary on the basis that the *-ā* infix is the agent pronoun (cf. ibid, 64: fol. 9a), and the pronoun is invariable.

5- naf^c alu:

The *na-* prefix is chosen in the imperfect's form *naf^c alu* of the 1st person of the pl. on the analogy of its choice as the first segment in the ending *-nā* of the perfect *fa^c al-nā* "we did" (cf. ibid, 66: fol. 10a).

1.7.1.1.2. The vowelling of the imperfect prefixes with a ḍamma:

The imperfect prefixes are vowelled by a ḍamma in the forms that are formed of four segments (cf. ibid, 68: fol. 10b), which are:

1- Form II of the triliteral: *fa^c^c ala* > *yu-fa^c^c ilu* [with double 2nd radical].

2- Form III of the triliteral: *fāᶜala > yu-fāᶜilu.*

3- Form IV of the triliteral: *ᵓafᶜala > yu-fᶜilu.*

Furthermore they are vowelled by a ḍamma in the passive voice Form I *yu-fᶜalu,* Form II *yu-faᶜᶜalu*, Form III *yu-fāᶜalu* etc.

1.7.1.1.3. The vowelling of the imperfect prefixes with a kasra:

The imperfect prefixes are vowelled by a kasra in the dialectal variant known as the *taltala* (cf. Rabin, 61). The following forms can be mentioned that take a kasra in this dialect:

1- Form I *faᶜila yafᶜalu,* namely *yifᶜalu* "you do" in which the imperfect prefix is given a kasra to conform it with the kasra of the 2nd radical of its perfect *faᶜila.* An example is *ᶜalima yaᶜlamu* "to know" in which the kasra of the imperfect prefixes gives notice of the kasra of the 2nd radical of the perfect *ᶜalima,* namely *ᵓi-ᶜlamu* "I know", *ti-ᶜlamu* "/2 masc. and 3 fem. sing.", *yi-ᶜlamu* "/3 masc. sing" and ni-ᶜlamu "/1st pl." (cf. Åkesson, *Ibn Masᶜūd* 68: fol. 10b).

2- Form V *tafaᶜᶜala ya-tafaᶜᶜalu*, namely in the 2nd person of the masc. sing. or the 3rd person of the fem. sing. *ti-tafaᶜᶜalu*, e.g. *ti-takallamu* "you talk or she talks" (cf. Volck/Kellgren, *Ibn Mālik* 11).

3- Form VII *ʾinfaʿala ya-nfaʿilu* namely in the 2nd person of the masc. sing. or the 3rd person of the fem. sing. *ti-nfaʿilu,* e.g. *ti-nṭaliqu* "you dash along or she dashes along" (cf. ibid).

4- Form X *ʾistafʿala ya-stafʿilu,* namely *yi-stafʿilu,* e.g. *ʾistanṣara ya-stanṣiru* "to ask for assistance", namely *yi-stanṣiru* "he asks for assistance", *ti-stanṣiru* "/2masc. sing." and "3 fem. sing.", *ʾi-stanṣiru* "/1 sing." and *ni-stanṣiru* "1 pl." (cf. Åkesson, *Ibn Masʿūd* 68: fol. 10b).

5- Form II of the quadriliteral *tafaʿlala ya-tafaʿlalu,* namely in the 2nd person of the masc. sing. or the 3rd person of the fem. sing. *ti-tafaʿlalu,* e.g. *ti-tadaḥrağu* "you roll along, or she rolls along" (cf. Volck/Kellgren, *Ibn Mālik* 11).

1.8. The imperative

The imperative, *al-ʾamr* is a mood through which the action is ordered from the subject. Its pattern is *ʾifʿal,* e.g. *ʾiḍrib* "hit!".

1.8a. The undeclinability of the imperative:

The imperative is undeclinable according to the Basrans (for their opinion see Ibn Ǧinnī, *Ḫaṣāʾiṣ III,* 83, Suyūṭī, *Ašbāh II,* 353-354). Its last radical is given the sukūn, which is a marker that is not given to the noun, - except in the pause which is a special case -, because its does not offer any similarity nor in meaning and nor in form, with the noun (cf. Ibn Yaʿīš, VII, 4).

However according to the Kufans the imperative is underlyingly declinable rather than undeclinable, as they only recognize the imperative as being a part of the declinable imperfect, as it is originally by them an imperfect preceded by the *li-* of command (for discussions see Ḥadīṯī, *Nuḥāt* 84). So the loss of the last vowel is a process which is similar to the case of the declinable imperfect that is put in the jussive mood when it follows the *li-* of the imperative, e.g. *li-yafʿal* "let him do" (cf. for the Kufans' opinion Farrāʾ, *Maʿānī I,* 491, Ṯaʿlab, *Maǧālis II,* 456; for the debate see Ibn al-Anbārī, *Inṣāf* Q. 72, 214-224, *Asrār* 125-126, Zamaḫšarī, 114-115, ʿUkbarī, *Masāʾil* 114-119, Ibn Yaʿīš, VII, 61-62).

1.8.1. The forms of the imperative:

The imperative is formed by eliding the li- of command together with the imperfect prefix of the 2nd persons. Then the connective hamza is prefixed instead of the imperfect prefix. Thus *li-taf*ᶜ*al* becomes ᵓ*if*ᶜ*al*, etc.

The forms of the imperative ᵓ*if*ᶜ*al* are the following:

	sing.	dual	pl.
2nd masc.	ᵓ*if*ᶜ*al*	ᵓ*if*ᶜ*al(a)-ā*	ᵓ*if*ᶜ*al(u)-ū*
2nd fem.	ᵓ*if*ᶜ*al(i)-ī*	ᵓ*if*ᶜ*al(a)-ā*	ᵓ*if*ᶜ*al-na*

The paradigm of Form I *ḍaraba* in the imperative is the following:

	sing.	dual	pl.
2nd masc.	ᵓ*iḍrib*	ᵓ*iḍrib(a)-ā*	ᵓ*iḍrib(u)-ū*
2nd fem.	ᵓ*iḍrib(i)-ī*	ᵓ*iḍrib(a)-ā*	ᵓ*iḍrib-na*

The *li-* of command and the vowelling of the connective hamza are discussed below.

1.8.1.1. The li- of command:

The *li–* of command that is followed by a verb in the jussive mood, e.g. *li-yafᶜal* "let him do!" resembles the preposition *li-* (cf. Åkesson, *Ibn Masᶜūd* 72: fol 12a) that is followed by a noun in the genitive, e.g. *li-Zaydin* "for Zayd" as both lāms are given a kasra. The verb in the jussive mood corresponds to the noun put in the genitive case (cf. Sībawaihi, I, 4). It can be remarked furthermore that nouns cannot be put in the jussive mood in the same manner as verbs cannot be put in the genitive case (cf. Carter, *Linguistics* [Širbīnī, *Āǧurrūmīya]* 40, 42).

The *li-* is made vowelless by the conjunction *wa-* e.g. *wa-l-yaḍrib* "and let him hit!" said instead of *wa-li-yaḍrib* and *fa-* e.g. *fa-l-yaḍrib* "then let him hit" said instead of *fa-li-yaḍrib* (cf. Åkesson, *Elision* 21).

1.8.1.2. The vowelling of the prefixed connective hamza of the imperative:

According to the Basrans the connective hamza is by principle given the kasra whereas according to the Kufans the connective hamza should follow in its vowel the vowel of the 2nd radical of the verb (for this debate see Ibn al-Anbārī, *Inṣāf* Q. 107, 309-312). According to others the connective prefixed hamza should by principle be vowelless because it is a prefix and it is prior to consider a prefix as being vowelless than vowelled (cf. ibid, Q. 107, 309-312).

The connective hamza is not given the kasra but a ḍamma when the 2nd radical is vowelled by a ḍamma, e.g. *ᵓuktub* "write!" and not *ᵓiktub,* for the sake of analogy (cf. Åkesson, *Ibn Masᶜūd* 74: fol. 12a).

1.9. The Energetic of the imperfect and of the imperative

The Energetic is formed by giving the termination *-anna* or *-an* to the imperfect jussive or to the imperative. The termination -*anna* refers to the Energetic I forms of the imperfect and imperative and the termination *-an* to the Energetic II forms of the imperfect and of the imperative. The Energetic is used to intensify the order in some cases, among which the following.

1- The imperative, e.g *ʾiḍribanna* "hit! /2 masc. sing. (imperative En. I.)" and *ʾiḍriban* (imperative En. II).

2- The prohibition, e.g. *lā taḍribanna* "do not hit!" (imperfect En. I.) and *lā taḍriban* "do not hit!" (imperfect En. II).

3- The interrogation, e.g. *hal taḍribanna* "will you hit?" (imperfect En. I.) and *hal taḍriban* (imperfect En. II).

4- The optative, e.g. *laytaka taḍribanna* "I wish you would hit" (imperfect En. I.) and *laytaka taḍriban* (imperfect En. II).

5- The request, e.g. *ʾalā taḍribanna* "are you not going to hit?" (imperfect En. I.) and *ʾalā taḍriban* (imperfect En. II).

6- The oath, e.g. *wa-l-lāhi lā taḍribanna* "by God, do not hit!" (imperfect En. I.) and *wa-l-lāhi lā taḍriban* (imperfect En. II).

The forms shall now be presented and discussed.

1.9.1. The forms of the Energetic:

The forms of the Energetic are divided between the Energetic I of the imperfect of the jussive *yafᶜala-nna,* the Energetic II of the imperfect of the jussive *yafᶜala-n*, the Energetic I of the imperative *ᵓifᶜala-nna* and the Energetic II of the imperative *ᵓifᶜala-n.*

1- The Energetic I of the imperfect of the jussive yafᶜala-nna:

The forms of the Energetic I of the imperfect of the jussive *yafᶜala-nna* are the following:

	sing.	dual	pl.
1st	*ᵓafᶜala-nna*		*nafᶜala-nna*
2nd masc.	*tafᶜala-nna*	*tafᶜal(a)-ānni*	*tafᶜalu-nna*
2nd fem.	*tafᶜali-nna*	*tafᶜal(a)-ānni*	*tafᶜal-n(a)ānni*
3rd masc.	*yafᶜala-nna*	*yafᶜal(a)-ānni*	*yafᶜalu-nna*
3rd fem.	*tafᶜala-nna*	*tafᶜal(a)-ānni*	*yafᶜal-n(a)ānni*

2- The Energetic II of the imperfect of the jussive yafᶜala-n:

The forms of the Energetic II of the imperfect of the jussive *yafᶜala-n* are the following:

	sing.	dual	pl.
1st	*ᵓafᶜala-n*		*nafᶜala-n*
2nd masc.	*tafᶜala-n*		*tafᶜalu-n*
2nd fem.	*tafᶜali-n*		
3rd masc.	*yafᶜala-n*		*yafᶜalu-n*
3rd fem.	*tafᶜala-n*		

3- The Energetic I of the imperative ᵓifᶜala-nna:

The forms of the Energetic I of the imperative *ᵓifᶜala-nna* are the following:

	sing.	dual	pl.
2nd masc	*ᵓifᶜala-nna*	*ᵓifᶜal(a)-ānni*	*ᵓifᶜalu-nna*
2nd fem..	*ᵓifᶜali-nna*	*ᵓifᶜal(a)-ānni*	*ᵓifᶜal-n(a)ānni*

4- The Energetic II of the imperative ʾifʿala-n:

The forms of the Energetic II of the imperative *ʾifʿala-n* are the following:

	sing.	dual	pl.
2nd masc	*ʾifʿala-n*		*ʾifʿalu-n*
2nd fem..	*ʾifʿali-n*		

1.9.1.2. Some remarks concerning some of the Energetic's forms:

The forms that are taken up at first are those to which the doubled or single *n* is suffixed to without the insertion of any infix or with the elision of one. In these cases, the Energetic's 3rd radical can be vowelled by a fatḥa as in the 3rd persons of the masc sing. *yafʿala-nna* and *yafʿala-n,* a ḍamma as in the 3rd persons of the masc pl. *yafʿalu-nna* and *yafʿalu-n* or a kasra as in the 2nd persons of the fem. sing. *tafʿali-nna, tafʿali-n, ʾifʿali-nna* and *ʾifʿali-n.* Then the forms with an infix preceding the doubled or single *n* together with a kasra vowelling the nūns instead of the fatḥa are discussed, as the infix *ā* of the dual of the 2nd persons of the dual *tafʿal(a)-ānni* and *ʾifʿal(a)-ānni,* and the inserted *ā* between the *-na* marker of the 3rd person of the fem. pl. and the doubled *n* in the 3rd person of the fem. pl. *yafᶜal-n(a)-ānni* and *ᵓifᶜal-n(a)-ānni.*

1- The 3rd persons of the masc sing.: yafᶜala-nna and yafᶜala-n:

The 3rd radical, which is vowelless in the imperfect jussive *li-yafᶜal* "let him do!" and in the imperative *ᵓifᶜal* "do!", is given a fatḥa when the doubled *n* of the Energetic I is suffixed to it. Hence *yafᶜala-nna* is said and not *yafᶜal-nna* to hinder the cluster of two vowelless segments (cf. Åkesson, *Ibn Masᶜūd* 76: fol. 13a). The form referring to the Energetic II with the suffixation of the single *n,* i.e. *yafᶜala-n*, follows it in its form.

2- The 3rd persons of the masc pl.: yafᶜalu-nna and yafᶜalu-n:

The *-ū* suffix of the masc. pl. which is added in the imperfect jussive *li-yafᶜal(u)-ū* "let them do!" and in the imperative *ᵓifᶜal(u)-ū* "do!", is elided when the doubled *n* of the Energetic I is suffixed to the form. Hence *yafᶜalu-nna* is said and not *yafᶜalu-(ū)nna* to alleviate. The form referring to the Energetic II with the suffixation of the single *n,* i.e. *yafᶜalu-n* follows it in its form.

3- The 2nd persons of the fem. sing.: tafᶜali-nna, tafᶜali-n, ᵓifᶜali-nna and ᵓifᶜali-n:

The *-ī* suffix of the fem. sing. which is added in the imperfect jussive *li-tafᶜal(i)-ī* "let her do!" and in the imperative *ᵓifᶜal(i)-ī* "do!", is elided when the doubled *n* of the Energetic I is suffixed to the form. Hence *tafᶜali-nna* is said and not *tafᶜali-(ī)nna* (cf. ibid), to alleviate. The forms referring to the Energetic II with the suffixation of the single *n,* i.e. *tafᶜali-n* and to the imperative Energetic I *ᵓifᶜali-nna* and Energetic II *ᵓifᶜali-n* follow it in their forms.

4- The 2nd persons of the dual: tafᶜal(a)-ānni and ᵓifᶜal(a)-ānni:

The *-ā* suffix of the dual which is added in the imperfect jussive *li-tafᶜal(a)-ā* "let her do!" and in the imperative *ᵓifᶜal(a)-ā* "do!", is not elided when the doubled *n* of the Energetic I is suffixed to the form. The reason of that is to avoid ambiguity with the sing. form (cf. Åkesson, *Ibn Masᶜūd* 76: fol. 13a) *yafᶜala-nna.* Another reason why the *-ā* is not elided is according to Ibn ᶜAqīl, II, 314, its lightness. Furthermore the double *n* is given a kasra and not a fatḥa because of its resemblance to the *n* given a kasra after the *ā* of the dual (cf. Åkesson, *Ibn Masᶜūd* 76: fols. 13a-13b) of the termination *-āni* added to the imperfect *yafᶜal(a)-āni.* Hence *tafᶜal(a)-ānni* is said and not *taf^cala-nna.* The form referring to the imperative Energetic I with the suffixation of the single *n,* i.e. *ʾif^cal(a)-ānni* follows it in its form.

The suffixation of the single *-n* is not carried out in the imperfect and in the imperative Energetic II to hinder the combination of the vowelless *ā* suffix of the dual and the vowelles single *-n* (cf. ibid, 76: fol. 13b). Hence the forms *taf^cal(a)-ān* and *ʾif^cal(a)-ān* are not existent by the majority of the grammarians, except by Yūnus and some of his Kufan followers (cf. Sībawaihi, II, 160, Ibn al-Sarrāǧ, *Uṣūl II,* 203, Ibn al-Anbārī, *Inṣāf* Q. 94, 271-277, Zamaḫšarī, 155, Ibn Ya^cīš, IX, 37-38, Ibn ^cAqīl, II, 315-316, Åkesson, *Ibn Mas^cūd* 76: fol. 13b).

<u>*5- The 3rd person of the fem. pl.: yaf^cal-n(a)-ānni and ʾif^cal-n(a)-ānni:*</u>

The *-ā* infix is inserted between the *-na* marker of the 3rd person of the fem. pl. and the doubled *n* to avoid the combination of the nūns (cf. Ibn ^cAqīl, II, 316, Åkesson, *Ibn Mas^cūd* 76: fol. 13b). Hence *yaf^cal-n(a)-ānni* is said and not *yaf^cal-n(a)-nni.* The form referring to the imperative Energetic I with the suffixation of the single *n,* i.e. *ʾif^cal-n(a)-ānni* follows it in its form.

The suffixation of the single *-n* is not carried out in this person in the imperfect and in the imperative Energetic II to hinder the combination of the inserted vowelless *ā* and the vowelles single *-n*. Hence *yafᶜal-n(a)-ān* and *ᵓifᶜal-n(a)-ān* are not existent.

1.10. The passive voice

The passive voice, *al-mağhūl* is the form of the verb that expresses the submission of the object to a certain action. The purpose of using it is either to express the baseness of the subject, its sublimity, celebrity, anonymity, the dread from it or the fearing for it.

Its pattern of the perfect is *fuᶜila* and of the imperfect *yufᶜalu.*

1.10.1. The patterns of the derived forms of the triliteral and Form I of the quadriliteral and its derived forms:

- Form II *fuᶜᶜila yufaᶜᶜalu,* e.g. "to be cut".

- Form III *fūᶜila yufāᶜalu,* e.g. *qūtila yuqātalu* "to be fought".

- Form IV *ᵓufᶜila yufᶜalu,* e.g. *ᵓukrima yukramu* "to be honoured".

- Form V *tufuᶜᶜila yutafᶜᶜalu,* e.g. *tuquttila yutaqattalu* "to be fought".

- Form VI *tufūᶜila yutafāᶜalu,* e.g. *tuqūtila yutaqātalu* "to be fought".

- Form VII *ᵓunfuᶜila yunfaᶜalu,* e.g. *ᵓunqutila yunqatalu* "to be killed".

- Form VIII *ʾuftuʿila yuftaʿalu,* e.g. *ʾuḥtuqira yuḥtaqaru* "to be despised".

- Form X *ʾustufʿila yustafʿalu,* e.g. *ʾustuḫriǧa yustaḫraǧu* "to be extracted".

As for Form I of the quadriliteral and the derived forms, they are the following:

- Form I *fuʿlila yufaʿlalu,* e.g. *duḥriǧa yudaḥraǧu* "to be rolled".

- Form II *tufuʿlila yutafaʿlalu,* e.g. *tuduḥriǧa yutadaḥraǧu,* e.g. "to be rolled along".

- Form III *ʾufʿunlila yufʿanlalu,* e.g. *ʾuḥrunǧima yuḥranǧamu* "to be gathered together in a mass".

- Form IV *ʾufʿulilla yufʿalallu,* e.g. *ʾuqšuʿirra yuqšaʿarru* "to be shuddered with horror".

1.11. The active participle

The active participle is a verbal adjective that denotes the "being of the subject" (Bohas/Kouloughli, *Linguistic* 76). It is derived from the imperfect (ibid, 75) because of a similarity that exists between them both.

The active participle has many Form I patterns, the most common among them being *fāᶜilun.*

After discussing the similarity of the active participle to the imperfect, Form I patterns of the triliteral together with the derived forms and Form I pattern of the quadriliteral together with the derived forms are discussed. Then the forms that present a similarity to the active participle, namely the assimilated adjective and the form which is derived from it, namely the elative, are taken up.

1.11a. The similarity of the active participle to the imperfect:

One similarity that has previously been taken up (cf. par. 1.7a.). is that the phonological forms of the imperfect *yaḍribu* and of the active participle *ḍ(a)āribun* are commensurable regarding the vowelling or the vowellessness of both these forms' respective consonants.

Another argument is that the active participle becomes similar to the imperfect in its reference to future time when it is used as a subject governing the noun after it in the accusative, as in e.g. *ᵓanā qātilun ġulāmaka* "I am going to kill your servant", which has the same meaning as *ᵓanā ᵓaqtulu ġulāmaka* or *sa-ᵓaqtulu ġulāmaka (cf.* Suyūṭī, *Ašbāh III,* 535-536). The active participle in the sense of the future that operates as a verb on the noun by putting it in the accusative, is also termed by the Kufans as *al-fiᶜlu l-dāᵓim* "the permansive verb", which has been criticized by the Basrans (for discussions including some references to some modern researchers who accept this term and others who refuse it see Rāğiḥī, *Farrāᵓ* 115-138).

1.11.1. The patterns of the groundform:

The forms that are presented are: 1- *fāᶜilun,* 2- *faᶜīlun* and 3- the forms of intensity.

1- *fāᶜilun:*

This form is derived from the form *yafᶜalu* in the imperfect by eliding the imperfect prefix, infixing the *ā* between the 1st and 2nd radical, and vowelling the 2nd radical with a kasra (cf. Åkesson, *Ibn Masᶜūd* 80: fol. 14b). An example is *ḍāribun* "hitting".

2- *fa^cīlun:*

The active participle can occur formed according to the pattern *fa^{c}īlun,* e.g. *naṣīrun* "helper".

One form is common for the masc. and fem. if the meaning is that of the passive participle *maf^{c}ūlun* (cf. Zamaḫšarī, 83, Ibn Ya^{c}īš, V, 102, Åkesson, *Ibn Mas^{c}ūd* 82: fol. 15b, de Sacy, I, 351-352, Wright, II, 186, Vernier, I, 368-369, Blachère, 114-116).

Examples are *qatīlun* "murdered" which is common for the masc. and fem. sing., on the basis that it refers to the passive participle masc. sing. *maqtūlu*n or to the fem. sing. *maqtūlatun* and *ğarīḥun* "wounded" that refers to the passive participle masc. sing. *mağrūḥun* or to the fem. sing. *mağrūḥatun.* This rule is broken if the form is taken as a substantive (cf. Åkesson, *Ibn Mas^{c}ūd* 82: fol. 15b, Vernier, I, 370, Wright, II, 186). Examples are *ḏabīḥatun* "a female victim" and *laqīṭatun* "a female foundling" which have a separate masc. form *ḏabīḥun* and *laqīṭun.*

An anomalous example is *qarībun* that is not formed according to the passive participle *maf^{c}ūlun,* but which in spite of this fact, is common for both the masc. and fem. as it is occurs instead of *qarībatun* in the sur. 7: 54 *$^\circ$inna raḥmata l-lāhi qarībun mina l-muḥsinīna* "Verily God's mercy is nigh unto them who do well" (cf. Zamaḫšarī, 83, Ibn Ya^cīš, V, 102, Åkesson, *Ibn Mas^cūd* 82: fol. 15b, Wright, II, 186).

3- The forms of intensity:

The most common form denoting intensification is *fa^cūlun* (cf. Åkesson, *Ibn Mas^cūd* 82: fol. 15b, Wright, II, 136), e.g. *manū^cun* "one who is offering great resistance".

The masc. and the fem. sing. have one common form if the pattern has the meaning of the active participle *fā^cilun* (cf. Åkesson, *Ibn Mas^cūd* 82: fol. 15b, Wright, II, 185, Fleisch, *Traité I,* 337). Examples are *^ɔimra^ɔatun ṣabūrun"* a patient woman" in whih *ṣabūrun* stands for the active participle *ṣābiratun* and *rağulun ṣabūrun* "a patient man" in which *ṣabūrun* stands for *ṣābirun.*

An anomalous case worth mentioning is *^caduwwatu*n "enemy" (underlyingly *^cad(u)ūatun* on the pattern *fa(u)ūlatun)* in the sentence *hiya ^caduwwatu l-lāhi* "she is God's enemy" that is on the pattern *fa^cūlun* which, on the basis that it has the meaning of the active participle *fā^cilun,* namely *^cādiyatun,* should not have a separate form for the fem. The reason however of its occurrence in the fem. according to the pattern *fa(u)ūlatun* is that it is compared to its contrary *ṣadīqatun* "friend /fem", which is on the pattern *fa^cīlun* (cf. Suyūṭī, *Ašbāh*

I, 422, Ibn Manẓūr, IV, 2848, Åkesson, *Ibn Mas*^{c}*ūd* 82: fol. 15b, Vernier, I, 369, Lane, II, 1980).

The pattern *fa*^{c}*ūlun* has a separate form for the fem. sing. if it has the meaning of the passive participle participle *maf*^{c}*ūlun,* e.g. *nāqatun ḥalūbatun* "a she-camel for milking" in which *ḥalūbatun* stands for the passive participle *maḥlūbatun.*

Some other forms of intensity are: *fa*^{cc}*ālun* (cf. Howell, I, fasc. IV, 1614), e.g. *ṣabbārun* "having an intense degree of patience", *mif*^{c}*alun* which is common to the instrumental noun and to the pattern that denotes the intensification of the active participle (cf. ibid, 1622), e.g. *miğḏamun* in the phrase *sayfun miğḏamun* "a sword which cuts off quickly", *mif*^{c}*ālun* that refers to one that is accustomed to the act, e.g. *misqāmun* "often diseased", *fi*^{cc}*īlun,* e.g. *fissīqun* "very sinful", *fu*^{cc}*ālun,* e.g. *kubbārun* "very large" and *ṭuwwālun* "very tall", *fa*^{cc}*ālatun,* e.g. ^{c}*allāmatun* "very learned" and nassābatun "a great genealogist", *fā*^{c}*ilatun,* e.g. *rāwiyatun* "one who hands down poems or historical facts by oral tradition", *fa*^{cc}*ūlatun,* e.g. *farrūqatun* "very timid", *fu*^{c}*alatun,* e.g. *ḍuḥakatun* "prone to laughter", *fu*^{c}*latun,* e.g. *ḍuḥkatun* "very ridiculous", *mif*^{c}*ālatun,* e.g. *miğḏāmatun* "a man who quickly cuts the tie of affection" and *mif*^{c}*īlun,* e.g. *mi*^{c}*ṭīrun* "one who uses much perfume".

The patterns *fa*^{cc}*ālatun, fā*^{c}*ilatun, fa*^{cc}*ūlatun, fu*^{c}*alatun, fu*^{c}*latun, mif*^{c}*ālatun, mif*^{c}*ālun* and *mif*^{c}*īlun* are common for both the masc. and fem. sing.

An anomalous example is *miskīnatun* "poor /fem. sing." which is formed according to the pattern *mif*^{c}*īlun* that should not have a separate form for the fem., but which in this case has. The reason is that it is compared to its contrary *faqīratun* "poor" which is formed according to the pattern *fa*^{c}*īlun* (cf. Sībawaihi, II, 218, Ibn Manẓūr, III, 2056, Åkesson, *Ibn Mas*^{c}*ūd* 82: fol. 15b, Lane, I, 1395, Vernier, I, 373-374).

1.11.2. The derived forms of the triliteral and Form I and the derived forms of the quadriliteral:

The active participle of the derived forms of the triliteral verb and Form I and the derived forms of the quadriliteral, is formed according to the form of the imperfect, by replacing the imperfect radical by the mīm vowelled by a ḍamma, namely *mu,* and by having the 2nd radical still vowelled by a kasra (cf. Åkesson, *Ibn Mas*^{c}*ūd* 82-84: fols 15b-16a, Vernier, I, 38, Wright, I, 300-301).

The following forms of the derived forms of the triliteral can be mentioned:

- Form II *yufa*^{cc}*ilu* > *mufa*^{cc}*ilun,* e.g. *yuqaṭṭi*^{c}*u* > *muqaṭṭi*^{c}*un* "cutting".

- Form III *yufā*^{c}*ilu* > *mufā*^{c}*ilun,* e.g. *yuqātilu* > *muqātilun* "fighting".

- Form IV *yuf*^{c}*ilu* > *muf*^{c}*ilun,* e.g. *yukrimu* > *mukrimun* "honouring".

- Form V *yatafa*^{cc}*alu* > *mutafa*^{cc}*ilun,* e.g. *yatafaḍḍalu* > *mutafaḍḍilun* "deigning".

- Form VI *yatafā*^{c}*alu* > *mutafā*^{c}*ilun,* e.g. *yataḍārabu* > *mutaḍāribun* "striking".

- Form VII *yanfa*^{c}*ilu* > *munfa*^{c}*ilun*, e.g. *yanṣarifu* > *munṣarifun* "departing".

- Form VIII *yafta*^{c}*ilu* > *mufta*^{c}*ilun,* e.g. *yaḥtaqiru* > *muḥtaqirun* "despising".

- Form X *yastaf*^{c}*ilu* > *mustaf*^{c}*ilun,* e.g. *yastaḫriğu* > *mustaḫriğun* "removing".

The following Form I of the quadriliteral and some of its derived forms can be mentioned:

- Form I *yufa*^{c}*lilu* > *mufa*^{c}*lilun,* e.g. *yudaḥriğu* > *mudaḥriğun* "rolling".

- Form II *yatafa*^{c}*lalu* > *mutafa*^{c}*lilun*, e.g. *yatadaḥrağu* > *mutadaḥriğun* "rolling along".

- Form III *yaf*^{c}*anlilu* > *muf*^{c}*anlilun,* e.g. *yaḥranğimu* > *muḥranğimun* "gathering together in a mass".

- Form IV *yafᶜalillu* > *mufᶜalillun,* e.g. *yaqšaᶜirru* > *muqšaᶜirrun* "shuddering with horror".

1.11.2.1. Some anomalous cases:

There exist some anomalous cases of active participles which are not formed according to the patterns of verbs to which they refer to.

An example is Form IV *mushabun* "loquacious in his speech" (cf. Ibn Manẓūr, III, 2131, Åkesson, *Ibn Masᶜūd* 84: fol. 16a, Lane, I, 1450) from Form IV *ᵓashaba* "to prolong in the speech", which is formed anomalously according to Form IV of the passive participle *mufᶜalun* instead of Form IV of the active participle *mufᶜilun.* Another example is *yāfiᶜun* "a grown-up boy" which is the active participle of the verb of Form IV *ᵓayfaᶜa* "to grow up" that is anomalously formed according to the form of the active participle of the verb of Form I *fāᶜilun* (cf. Ibn Manẓūr, VI, 4963, Åkesson, *Ibn Masᶜūd* 84: fol. 16a, Vernier, I, 169).

1.12. The assimilated adjective

The assimilated adjective, *al-ṣifa al-mušabbaha* is the adjective that is assimilated to the participles on the basis of its inflection. Its patterns are derived from Form I of the triliteral verb. Some of the principal measures with some examples are the following:

1- *faᶜlun* e.g. *šaksun* "perverse, stubborn".

2- *faᶜalun* e.g. *ḥasanun* "handsome".

3- *faᶜilun* e.g. *fariqun* "fearful" and *ḫašinun* "rough".

4- *fiᶜlun* e.g. *milḥun* "witty".

5- *fuᶜlun* e.g. *ṣulbun* "hard, rigid".

6- *fuᶜulun* e.g. *ǧunubun* "polluted".

7- *fuᶜālun* e.g. *šuǧāᶜun* "courageous".

8- *faᶜlānun* e.g. *ᶜaṭšānun* "thirsty" and *ǧabānun* "coward".

9- *ᵓafᶜalu* e.g. *ᵓaḥwalu* "squinting". This pattern can present forms that are derived either from the conjugation *faᶜila* as the mentioned *ᵓaḥwalu,* or from the dialectal variants *faᶜula* (cf. Zabīdī, *Tāǧ XXIV,* 124, Åkesson, *Ibn Masᶜūd* 80: fol. 14b-15a) or *faᶜila,* e.g. *ᵓaḥmaqu* "foolish" from *ḥamuqa / ḥamiqa, ᵓaḫraqu* "unskillful" from *ḫaruqa / ḫariqa, ᵓādamu* "brown" from *ᵓaduma / ᵓadima, ᵓarᶜanu* "careless, silly" from *raᶜuna / raᶜina, ᵓasmaru* "brown" from *samura / samira, ᵓaᶜǧafu* "lean, meagre" from *ᶜağufa / ᶜağifa* and *ʾaᶜğamu* "non-Arab, dumb, speechless" from *ᶜağuma / ᶜağima* (cf. Astarābāḏī, *Šarḥ al-šāfiya I,* 71).

1.13. The elative form *ʾafᶜalu*

The elative, *ism al-tafḍīl* is an adjective that denotes the superiority of the active participle. Its form is *ʾafᶜalu.*

It is derived from Form I of the triliteral, active, *faᶜala* (cf. Åkesson, *Ibn Masᶜūd* 80: fol. 15a, ᶜAbd al-Raḥīm, *Ṣarf* 96).

1.13.1. Some anomalous cases:

Some anomalies occur concerning the elative. It is not to be derived from the following forms, namely:

1- from the passive voice's form *fuᶜila.* An anomalous example is however *ʾazhā,* which is derived from the passive voice *zuhiya,* in the expression *huwa ʾazhā min dīkin* "he is more self conceited than a cock" (cf. Zamaḫšarī, 102, Howell, I, fasc. IV, 1703, Vernier, I, 230).

2- from the passive participle's form, *mafᶜūlun* because the elative is meant to refer to the agent and not the object (cf. Åkesson, *Ibn Masᶜūd* 80-82: fol. 15a). Some anomalies exist as the adjective *ʾašġalu* derived from the passive participle *mašġūlun* "busy" that is used as an elative in the proverb *ʾašġalu min ḏāti l-naḥiyayni* (cf. Zamaḫšarī, 102, Åkesson, *Ibn Masᶜūd* 82: fol. 15a, Freytag, *Proverbia* 687, Lane, I, 1567, Bustānī, *Muḥīṭ* 471).

3- from the verbal adjective's form that denotes colors *ᵓafᶜalu,* e.g. *ᵓaḥmaru* "red", as it is not said *ᵓaḥmaru min* "more red than", to avoid ambiguity. The Kufans however allow the elative to be formed of the colors *bayāḍun* "whiteness" and *sawādun* "blackness", i.e. *ᵓabyaḍu min* "whiter than" and *ᵓaswadu min* "blacker than", whereas the Basrans do not allow it (for the debate see Ibn al-Anbārī, *Inṣāf* Q. 16, 68-70).

4- from the verbal adjective's form that denotes deformities *ᵓafᶜalu,* e.g. *ᵓaᶜwaru* "one-eyed", as it is not said *ᵓaᶜwaru min* "more one eyed than", to avoid ambiguity. Some anomalies occur however as the example of the adjective *ᵓaḥmaqu* "stupid" which occurs as an elative in the proverb *ᵓaḥmaqu min Habannaqah* "more stupid than Habannaqah"(cf. Zamaḫšarī, 102, Åkesson, *Ibn Masᶜūd* 82: fol. 15a, Freytag, *Proverbia II,* 392).

5- from the derived patterns of the triliteral verb because it would be impossible to maintain all of its segments within the pattern *ᵓafᶜalu* (cf. Åkesson, *Ibn Masᶜūd* 80: fol. 15a). Some anomalous cases however exist as the elatives *ᵓaᶜṭā* "the one who gives more freely" and *ᵓawlā* "the one who bestows more liberally", which are formed anomalously from Form IV *ᵓaᶜṭā* "to give" and *ᵓawlā* "to entrust" respectively. They both occur in the example *huwa ᵓaᶜṭāhum wa-ᵓawlāhum* "he is the one among them who gives more freely and bestows more liberally" (cf. ibid 82: fol. 15a). Other examples occur in the sur. 2: 282

(ḏālikum ᵓaqsaṭu ᶜinda l-lāhi wa-ᵓaqwamu li-l-šahādati) "It is juster in the sight of God, more suitable as evidence, and more convenient to prevent doubts among yourselves", in which *ᵓaqsaṭu* is formed anomalously from Form IV *ᵓaqsaṭa* "to act justly" and *ᵓaqwamu* from Form IV *ᵓaqāma* "to make right".

1.14. The passive participle

The passive participle, *ʾism al-maf^{c}ūl*, is a verbal noun which is derived from the passive voice of the imperfect *yu-f^{c}alu* (cf. Åkesson, *Ibn Mas^{c}ūd* 86: fol. 16a). It denotes the object on whom or on which the act falls upon.

Its pattern in Form I of the triliteral is *maf^{c}ūlun,* e.g. *maḍrūbun* "he/it is hit /masc. sing.". Its form of the derived patterns of the triliteral and of Form I of the quadriliteral and its derived forms is formed according to the pattern of the imperfect of the passive voice of the implied form, by replacing the imperfect prefix by the *m* vowelled by a ḍamma, i.e. *mu* (for examples see Wright, II, 300-301, Vernier, I, 166-167).

Hence the following forms:

- Form II *yufa^{cc}alu* > *mufa^{cc}alun,* e.g. *yuqaṭṭa^{c}u* > *muqaṭṭa^{c}un* "cut".

- Form III *yufā^{c}alu* > *mufā^{c}alun,* e.g. *yuqātalu* > *muqātalun* "fought".

- Form IV *yuf^{c}alu* > *muf^{c}alun,* e.g. *yukramu* > *mukramun* "honoured".

- Form V *yutafa^{cc}alu* > *mutafa^{cc}alun.*

- Form VI *yutafā^{c}alu* > *mutafā^{c}alun.*

- Form VII *yunfa^{c}alu* > *munfa^{c}alun.*

- Form VIII *yufta^{c}alu* > *mufta^{c}alun,* e.g. *yuḥtaqaru* > *muḥtaqarun* "despised".

- Form X *yustaf^{c}alu* > *mustaf^{c}alun,* e.g. *yustaḫrağu* > *mustaḫrağun* "removed".

As for the groundform and some of the derived forms of the quadriliteral of the verbs the following forms may be presented:

- Form I *yufa^{c}lalu* > *mufa^{c}lalun,* e.g. *yudaḥrağu* > *mudaḥrağun* "rolled".

- Form II *yutafa^{c}lalu* > *mutafa^{c}lalun,* e.g. *yutadaḥrağu* > *mutadaḥrağun* "rolled along".

- Form III *yuf^{c}anlalu* > *muf^{c}anlalun.*

- Form IV *yuf^{c}alallu* > *muf^{c}alallun.*

1.15. The nouns of time and place

The nouns of time and place, *ʾasmāʾ al-zamān wa-l-makān*, are verbal nouns that denote the time or place with respect to the occurrence of the act therin.

Their patterns are divided between *mafʿalun* and *mafʿilun.*

An example of the pattern *mafʿalun* is *maḏhabun* "a place of departure".

The following nouns are formed according to the pattern *mafʿilun* (for a presentation see Zamaḫšarī, 104, Åkesson, *Ibn Masʿūd* 88: fol. 17a, Wright, II, 125-126, Vernier, I, 189, Blachère, 95):

1- *mansikun* "a place where a sacrifice is offered during a religious festival". It can be noted that both *mansikun* with the *s* vowelled by a kasra and *mansakun* with it vowelled by a fatḥa have been read of the sur. 22: 67 *(ǧaʿalnā mansikan)* or *(ǧaʿalnā mansakan)* "Have We appointed rites and ceremonies" (cf. Muʾaddib, *Taṣrīf* 124, Ibn Manẓūr, VI, 4412).

2- *maǧzirun* "a place where animals are slaughtered, slaughterhouse".

3- *manbitun* "a place where a plant grows".

4- *maṭliʿun* "a place of ascent or rising". Both variants *maṭliʿun* with the kasra given to the ṭ and *maṭlaʿun* with the fatḥa given to it exist. The variant *maṭli^{c}un* is said to be of the dialect of Tamīm and *maṭla^{c}un* is said to be of the dialect of the Ḥiğāzis (cf. Sībawaihi, II, 264, Volck/Kellgren: *Ibn Mālik* 24, Ibn Manẓūr, VI, 2689).

5- *mašriqun* "a place where the sun rises, the east".

6- *maġribun* "a place where the sun sets, the west".

7- *mafriqun* "a place of division, the crown of the head".

8- *masqiṭun* "a place where anything falls".

9- *maskinun* "a place where one dwells, habitation".

10- *marfiqun* "a place on which one rests, the elbow".

11- *masğidun* "a place of prostration in prayer, a mosque".

12- *manḫirun* "a place where the breath passes through the nose".

The noun of time is similar to the noun of place, e.g. *maqtalu l-Ḥusayn* "the time or place of killing Ḥusain".

1.16. The noun of instrument

The noun of instrument, *ʾism al-ʾāla,* is derived from the imperfect. It denotes the instrument that is used in carrying out the action expressed by the verb. Its common patterns are the following:

1- *mifʿalun,* e.g. *mibradun* "a file".

2- *mifʿālun,* e.g. *miftāḥun* "a key".

3- *mifʿalatun,* e.g. *miknasatun* "a broom".

4- *mufʿulun,* e.g. *musʿuṭun* "an instrument for introducing medicine into the nose" *munḫulun* "a sieve", *mudhunun* "a thing [or pot or vase] in which oil, flash or phial was put" and *muduqqun* "a thing with which one bruises, brays or pounds".

Instrumental nouns are also formed on the measure of *mifʿalun* or *mifʿalatun.* Hence, the nouns *miǧrafatun, miḥassatun* and *miqraʿatun* combined together formed upon the measure *mifʿalatun* occur in a verse said by al-Farazdaq in an elegy on a groom, cited by Howell, I, fasc. IV, 1757:

"Li-yabki ʾabā l-Ḫansāʾi baġlun wa-baġlatun
wa-miḫlātu sawʾin qad ʾuḍīʿa šaʿīruhā
wa-miǧrafatun maṭrūḥatun wa-miḥassatun
wa-miqraʿatun ṣafrāʾu bālin suyūruhā".
"Let a he-mule, and a she-mule, and a nose-bag of evil,

whose barley has been wasted, and a rejected broom,
and a curry comb, and a yellow whip whose thongs are
worn out, bewail Abū l-Ḫansāᵓ".

Instrumental nouns of the measure *mufᶜulatun* and *mifᶜulatun* exist as well, but they are said to be anomalous, e.g. *al-mukḥulatu* "a thing in which there is a preparation of pulverized antimony used for darkening the edges of the eyelids" (cf. Sībawaihi, II, 265) and *al-miḥruḍatu* "a vessel made of wood, or of brass" (cf. Ibn Manẓūr, II, 837, Lane, I, 549.

2. THE CLASS OF THE DOUBLED VERB

The doubled verb, *al-muḍāᶜaf,* is the verb in which the 2nd and 3rd radicals are identical segments. It is also termed as *al-ᵓaṣamm* "the solid verb" because of its *šadda* as both the 2nd and 3rd radical are assimilated together.

2.1. The conjugations of the doubled verb

The doubled verb falls into four conjugations, of which the fourth occurs very rarely:

1- *fa^{c}ala yaf^{c}ulu,* e.g. *sarara yasruru* "to gladden" that becomes after the assimilation *sarra yasurru.*

2- *fa^{c}ala yaf^{c}ilu,* e.g. *farara yafriru* "to escape" that becomes after the assimilation *farra yafirru.*

3- *fa^{c}ila yaf^{c}alu,* e.g. *^{c}aḍiḍa ya^{c}ḍaḍu* "to bite" that becomes after the assimilation *^{c}aḍḍa ya^{c}aḍḍu.*

4- *fa^{c}ula yaf^{c}ulu.* Only a few verbs seem to be formed according to this conjugation. Some examples are *ḥabuba yaḥbubu* that becomes after the assimilation *ḥabba yaḥubbu* "to love", *labuba yalbubu* that becomes *labba yalubbu.* Other examples are *sarura* "to become evil", *ramuma* "to repair" and *ḫafufa* "to be light".

2.2. Examples of some derivatives and paradigms of the doubled verb

An example of a doubled verb in the perfect is *madda* "to stretch" underlyingly *madada.* It becomes *yamuddu* in the imperfect of the indicative active. Its imperative is *mudd,* its active participle is *māddun,* its *maṣdar* is *maddun,* its perfect passive is *mudda,* its imperfect is *yumaddu,* its passive participle is *mamdūdun,* its nouns of time and place are *mamaddun* and the noun of instrument is *mimaddun.*

Its paradigm in the perfect, active, is as follows:

	sing.	dual	pl.
1st	*madad-tu*		*madad-n(a)ā*
2nd masc.	*madad-ta*	*madad-tum(a)ā*	*madad-tum*
2nd fem.	*madad-ti*	*madad-tum(a)ā*	*madad-tunna*
3rd masc.	*madda*	*madd(a)-ā*	*madd(u)-ū*
3rd fem.	*madda-t*	*madda-t(a)ā*	*madad-na*

Its imperfect in the indicative, active, is the following:

	sing.	dual	pl.
1st	*ᵓamuddu*		*namuddu*
2nd masc.	*tamuddu*	*tanudd(a)-āni*	*tamudd(u)-ūna*
2nd fem.	*tamudd(i)-īna*	*tamudd(a)-āni*	*tamdud-na*
3rd masc.	*yamuddu*	*yamudd(a)-āni*	*yamudd(u)-ūna*
3rd fem.	*tamuddu*	*tamudd(a)-āni*	*yamdud-na*

<u>Its imperfect in the indicative, subjunctive, is the following:</u>

	sing.	dual	pl.
1st	*ʾamudda*		*namuddu*
2nd masc.	*tamudda*	*tanudd(a)-ā*	*tamudd(u)-ū*
2nd fem.	*tamudd(i)-ī*	*tamudd(a)-ā*	*tamdud-na*
3rd masc.	*yamudda*	*yamudd(a)-ā*	*yamudd(u)-ū*
3rd fem.	*tamuddu*	*tamudd(a)-ā*	*yamdud-na*

<u>Its imperfect in the indicative, jussive, is the following:</u>

	sing.	dual	pl.
1st	*ʾamudd*		*namudd*
	or		or
	ʾamdud		*namdud*
2nd masc.	*tamudd*	*tamudd(a)-ā*	*tamudd(u)-ū*
	or		
	tamdud		
2nd fem.	*tamudd(i)-ī*	*tamudd(a)-ā*	*tamdud-na*
3rd masc.	*yamudd*	*yamudd(a)-ā*	*yamudd(u)-ū*
	or		
	yamdud		
3rd fem.	*tamudd*	*tamudd(a)-ā*	*yamdud-na*
	or		
	tamdud		

B- The paradigm of *farra* (to escape) in the perfect, active, (of which the imperfect is *yafirru* with the imperfect's 2nd radical's vowel being a kasra), is the following:

	sing.	dual	pl.
1st	*farar-tu*		*farar-n(a)ā*
2nd masc.	*farar-ta*	*farar-tum(a)ā*	*farar-tum*
2nd fem.	*farar-ti*	*farar-tum(a)ā*	*farar-tunna*
3rd masc.	*farra*	*farr(a)-ā*	*farr(u)-ū*
3rd fem.	*farra-t*	*farra-t(a)ā*	*farar-na*

Its imperfect in the indicative, active, is the following:

	sing.	dual	pl.
1st	*ʾafirru*		*nafirru*
2nd masc.	*tafirru*	*tafirr(a)-āni*	*tafirr(u)-ūna*
2nd fem.	*tafirr(i)-īna*	*tafirr(a)-āni*	*tafrir-na*
3rd masc.	*yafirru*	*yafirr(a)-āni*	*yafirr(u)-ūna*
3rd fem.	*tafirru*	*tafirr(a)-āni*	*yafrir-na*

Its imperfect in the indicative, subjunctive, is the following:

	sing.	dual	pl.
1st	*ʾafirra*		*nafirra*
2nd masc.	*tafirra*	*tafirr(a)-ā*	*tafirr(u)-ū*
2nd fem.	*tafirr(i)-ī*	*tafirr(a)-ā*	*tafrir-na*
3rd masc.	*yafirra*	*yafirr(a)-ā*	*yafirr(u)-ū*
3rd fem.	*tafirr*	*tafirr(a)-ā*	*yafrir-na*

Its imperfect in the indicative, jussive, is the following:

	sing.	dual	pl.
1st	*ʾafirr* or *ʾafrir*		*nafirr* or *nafrir*
2nd masc.	*tafirr* or *tafrir*	*tafirr(a)-ā*	*tafirr(u)-ū*
2nd fem.	*tafirr(i)-ī*	*tafirr(a)-ā*	*tafrir-na*
3rd masc.	*yafirr* or *yafrir*	*yafirr(a)-ā*	*yafirr(u)-ū*
3rd fem.	*tafirr* or *tafrir*	*tafirr(a)-ā*	*yafrir-na*

C- The paradigm of *ᶜaḍḍa* (to bite) in the perfect, active, (of which the imperfect is *yaᶜaḍḍu* with the imperfect's 2nd radical's vowel being a fatḥa), is the following:

	sing.	dual	pl.
1st	*ᶜaḍiḍ-tu*		*ᶜaḍiḍ-n(a)ā*
2nd masc.	*ᶜaḍiḍ-ta*	*ᶜaḍiḍ-tum(a)ā*	*ᶜaḍiḍ-tum*
2nd fem.	*ᶜaḍiḍ-ti*	*ᶜaḍiḍ-tum(a)ā*	*ᶜaḍiḍ-tunna*
3rd masc.	*ᶜaḍḍa*	*ᶜaḍḍ(a)-ā*	*ᶜaḍḍ(u)-ū*
3rd fem.	*ᶜaḍḍa-t*	*ᶜaḍḍa-t(a)ā*	*ᶜaḍiḍ-na*

Its imperfect in the indicative, active, is the following:

	sing.	dual	pl.
1st	*ᵓaᶜaḍḍu*		*naᶜaḍḍu*
2nd masc.	*taᶜaḍḍu*	*taᶜaḍḍ(a)-āni*	*taᶜaḍḍ(u)-ūna*
2nd fem.	*taᶜaḍḍ(i)-īna*	*taᶜaḍḍ(a)-āni*	*taᶜḍad-na*
3rd masc.	*yaᶜaḍḍu*	*yaᶜaḍḍ(a)-āni*	*yaᶜaḍḍ(u)-ūna*
3rd fem.	*taᶜaḍḍu*	*taᶜaḍḍ(a)-āni*	*yaᶜḍad-na*

<u>Its imperfect in the indicative, subjunctive, is the following:</u>

	sing.	dual	pl.
1st	*ʾaᶜaḍḍa*		*naᶜaḍḍa*
2nd masc.	*taᶜaḍḍa*	*taᶜaḍḍ(a)-ā*	*taᶜaḍḍ(u)-ū*
2nd fem.	*taᶜaḍḍ(i)-ī*	*taᶜaḍḍ(a)-ā*	*taᶜḍad-na*
3rd masc.	*yaᶜaḍḍa*	*yaᶜaḍḍ(a)-ā*	*yaᶜaḍḍ(u)-ū*
3rd fem.	*taᶜaḍḍa*	*taᶜaḍḍ(a)-ā*	*yaᶜḍad-na*

<u>Its imperfect in the indicative, jussive, is the following:</u>

	sing.	dual	pl.
1st	*ʾaᶜaḍḍ* or *ʾaᶜḍad*		*naᶜaḍḍ* or *naᶜḍad*
2nd masc.	*taᶜaḍḍ* or *taᶜḍad*	*taᶜaḍḍ(a)-ā*	*taᶜaḍḍ(u)-ū*
2nd fem.	*taᶜaḍḍ(i)-ī*	*taᶜaḍḍ(a)-ā*	*taᶜḍad-na*
3rd masc.	*yaᶜaḍḍ* or *yaᶜḍad*	*yaᶜaḍḍ(a)-ā*	*yaᶜaḍḍ(u)-ū*
3rd fem.	*taᶜaḍḍ* or *taᶜḍad*	*taᶜaḍḍ(a)-ā*	*yaᶜḍad-na*

2.2.1. Remarks concerning the phonological procedures in some of its forms:

A few representative forms are selected below with the aim of underlining on the one hand the sequences that lead to the assimilation or to any other phonological procedure, and on the other hand, those that prohibit any possible change. Each of the presented sequences is formed of two identical segments that can either be vowelled or vowelless. It goes without saying that two vowelless segments cannot be combined together. The presentation of these sequences will enable me to discuss the rules determining these procedures.

As it shall be remarked, the assimilation is not carried out in all the forms of the doubled verb and some of its derivatives. There exist some forms in which the assimilation of the two identical segments is prohibited. A few examples are the forms of the perfect, imperfect and imperative in which the vowelled pronoun of the agent is suffixed, e.g. the perfect *madad-tu* "I stretched", the imperfect *tamdud-na* "you stretch /fem. pl." and the imperative *ʾumdud-na* "stretch!" (cf. 2.2.1.3.).

Other forms are affected by the following changes:

1) the assimilation of the identical segments that is carried out in the perfect, e.g. *sarra* from *sarara* "he gladdened", in the

imperfect *yasurru* from *yasruru* "he gladdens" (cf. 2.2.1.2.) and in some cases of anomalous imperatives, e.g. *mudda, muddi* and *muddu* from *ᵓumdud* "stretch! /2nd person of the masc. sing." (cf. 2.2.1.5.).

2) the elision of one of the identical segments in some cases of anomalous perfects, e.g. *ẓal-ta* from *ẓalil-ta* "you continued" (cf. 2.2.1.4.).

3) the substitution of one of the segments by a *y* in some cases of derived forms of the doubled verb, e.g. *taẓannay-tu* from *taẓannan-tu* "I formed an opinion" (cf. 2.2.1.7.).

The forms and sequences that are selected are the following:

2.2.1.1. The verbal noun: the sequence of two identical segments of which the 1st is vowelless and the 2nd is vowelled: the assimilation.

2.2.1.2. The perfect and the imperfect: the sequence of two vowelled identical segments: the assimilation.

2.2.1.3. The forms of the perfect, imperfect and imperative in which the vowelled pronoun of the agent is suffixed: the sequence of a vowelled segment preceding a vowelless identical segment: the prohibition of the assimilation.

2.2.1.4. Some cases of anomalous perfects: the sequence of a vowelled segment preceding a vowelless identical segment: the elision of one of the identical segments.

2.2.1.5. Some cases of anomalous imperatives: the sequence of a vowelled segment preceding a vowelless identical segment: the assimilation.

2.2.1.6. Some cases of anomalous imperatives: the sequence of a vowelled segment preceding a vowelless identical segment: the elision of one of the identical segments.

2.2.1.7. Some derived forms of the verb: the sequence of a vowelled segment preceding a vowelless identical segment: the substitution of one of the doubled segments by a *y*.

2.2.1.1. The verbal noun: the sequence of two identical segments of which the 1st is vowelless and the 2nd is vowelled: the assimilation:

The phonological procedure that can be carried out in a word in which the sequence invoved is that of a vowelless segment preceding a vowelled identical segment is the assimilation of the first segment to the second. An example of such a case is the verbal noun *maddun* "an extension" (مَدْدٌ)، which is formed according to the pattern *fa^clun,* with two dāls written of which the 1st *d* is vowelless and the 2nd is vowelled. After the assimilation of the dāls it becomes *maddun* with the doubled *d* referred to in Arabic by the *d* carrying the *šadda:* (مَدٌّ) .

2.2.1.2. The perfect and the imperfect: the sequence of two vowelled identical segments: the assimilation:

The common procedure that can affect the stucture of the doubled verb in which the sequence invoved is that of two vowelled identical segments is the assimilation of both the identical vowelled segments.

In Form I of the 3rd person of the perfect of the doubled verb in which the assimilation is carried out, the vowel of the 2nd radical is dropped and the 2nd radical is assimilated to the 3rd. Thus:

sarara → *sarra* "he gladdened"

farara → *farra* "he escaped"

ᶜaḍiḍa → *ᶜaḍḍa* "he bit"

ḥabuba → *ḥabba* "he loved"

As what concerns its imperfect, the phonological procedure that is observed is that the vowel of the 2nd radical is not dropped but switched to the 1st vowelless radical and the 2nd radical is assimilated to the 3rd:

yasruru → *yasurru* "he gladdens"

yafriru → *yafirru* "he escapes"

yaᶜḍadu → *yaᶜaḍḍu* "he bites"

yaḥbubu → *yaḥubbu* "he loves"

The following variations occur concerning the verbs *radda, farra* and *ᶜaḍḍa* (for them see Howell, IV, fasc. II, 1699). Asad and some other people say *rudda, firra* and *ᶜaḍḍa* by vowelling the 1st radical with a ḍamma, kasra or fatḥa respectively and by assimilating the 2nd radical to the 3rd vowelled by a fatḥa. Kaᶜb and Numair say *ruddi, firri* and *ᶜaḍḍi* by vowelling the 1st radical with a ḍamma, kasra or fatḥa respectively and by assimilating the 2nd radical to the 3rd radical vowelled with the kasra. Other variants pertaining to their dialect are *ruddu, firri* and *ᶜaḍḍa* with the alliteration of the vowel of the 1st radical and with the 2nd radical assimilated to the 3rd that is given the same vowel as the 1st radical's vowel.

2.2.1.3. The forms of the perfect, imperfect and imperative in which the vowelled pronoun of the agent is suffixed: the sequence of a vowelled segment preceding a vowelless identical segment: the prohibition of the assimilation:

As a general rule, the sequence of a vowelled segment preceding a vowelless segment prevents in most cases the assimilation.

In the forms of the doubled verb occurring in the perfect, imperfect and imperative in which the vowelled agent pronouns are suffixed, the 3rd radical becomes vowelless to prevent the disliked succession of four vowelled segments. Hence the sequence is that of a vowelled segment preceding a vowelless segment.

In the case of the perfect, the vowelled agent pronouns are the *-tu* "/1st person of the sing.", the *-ta* "2nd person of the masc. sing.", the *-ti* "2nd person of the fem sing., the *-n(a)ā* "1st person of the pl.", the *-tum* "2nd person of the masc. pl.", the *-tunna* "2nd person of the fem. pl." and the *-na* "3rd person of the fem. pl.". Hence the forms implied for instance by the example *madada* "to stretch" are: *madad-tu, madad-ta, madad-ti, madad-n(a)ā, madad-tum, madad-tunna* and *madad-na* which all occur with the elision of the fatḥa from the 2nd *d* of *madada.*

The vowelled agent suffix pronoun in the cases of the imperfect and of the imperative is the *-na.* It marks the 2nd and 3rd person of the fem. pl. in the case of the imperfect, namely *tamdud-na* "you stretch /fem. pl." and *yamdud-na* "they stretch /fem. pl." respectively, and the 2nd person of the fem. pl. in the case of the imperative, namely *ʾumdud-na* "stretch!". In all these cases the assimilation of the two identical segments, namely the 2nd radical vowelled *d,* the *du,* to the 3rd radical vowelless *d* is forbidden because of the vowellessness of this 2nd *d* that has lost its vowel in order to prevent the succession of the vowels when the suffixed *-na* of the fem. pl. is suffixed to the word, and because this vowellessness marks as well the imperative.

2.2.1.4. Some cases of anomalous perfects: the sequence of a vowelled segment preceding a vowelless identical segment: the elision of one of the identical segments:

The sequence of a vowelled segment preceding a vowelless segment allows in some anomalous cases the elision of one of the identical segments.

In some anomalous cases of verbs occurring in the perfect in which one of the vowelled pronouns of the agent is suffixed to, the elision of one of the identical segments can be carried out.

An example is *ẓalil-ta* "you continued all day /masc. sing." and *ẓalil-ti* "you continued all day /fem. sing.", with the 3rd radical *l* made vowelless on account of the suffixation of the vowelled agent pronoun in order to prevent the succession of four vowels. This sequence of a vowelled segment, namely the vowelled 2nd radical *l,* preceding a vowelless identical segment, namely the vowelless 3rd radical *l,* forbids the assimilation. The elision of one of the lāms is carried out by some, which implies that *ẓalil-ta* and *ẓalil-ti* become *ẓal-ta* or *ẓal-ti* respectively (cf. Ibn Mālik, *La Alfīya* 222, Ibn ᶜAqīl, II, 584, Åkesson, *Ibn Masᶜūd* 196: fol. 18b, Wright, II, 69, Howell, IV, fasc. II, 1836 sqq., de Sacy, I, 228). The alleviated form *ẓalta* occurs in the sur. 20: 97 *(l-laḏī ẓalta ᶜalayhi ᶜākifan)* "Of whom thou hast become a devoted worshipper", and *ẓaltum* in the sur. 56: 65 *(fa-ẓaltum tafakkahūna)* "And ye would be left in wonderment" (cf. Howell, IV, fasc. II, 1836).

2.2.1.5. Some cases of anomalous imperatives: the sequence of a vowelled segment preceding a vowelless identical segment: the assimilation:

In some cases of doubled verbs occurring in the imperative, the assimilation of the identical segments is carried out in spite of the vowelless state of the 2nd segment following a vowelless segment, which by principle should prevent the assimilation.

An example is the imperative of the 2nd person of the masc. sing. *ᵓumdud* "stretch!" with the 1st *d* vowelled by a ḍamma and the 2nd *d* vowelless, which becomes *mudda, muddi* and *muddu* (cf. Åkesson, *Ibn Masᶜūd* 196: fol. 18b, Wright, II, 70). Those who dissolute are the Ḥiǧāzīs whereas those who assimilate are the people of Tamīm (cf. Wright, II, 70 in the notes).

By contrast to the variant of the imperative of the 2nd person of the masc. sing. *muddu* in which the ḍamma is given to the *d* on the analogy of the ḍamma of the 1st radical *m* (cf. Åkesson, *Ibn Masᶜūd* 196: fol. 18b), it is impossible to use the variant *firru* "flee!" for the imperative of the 2nd person of the masc. sing. of *farra* "to flee", with the ḍamma vowelling the *r* instead of the usual form *ᵓifrir,* as the ḍamma is disliked after the kasra of the 1st radical (cf. ibid). However *firra* and *firri* are possible variants to be used instead of *ᵓifrir,* with the fatḥa and the kasra vowelling the r respectively (cf. de Sacy, I, 229, Wright, II, 70), as *mudda* and *muddi* mentioned above.

Both *ᶜaḍḍa* and *ᶜaḍḍi* are used as well as variants with the assimilation of the ḍāds instead of *ᵓiᶜḍaḍ* bite! /masc. sing. (cf. Wright, II, 70).

2.2.1.6. Some cases of anomalous imperatives: the sequence of a vowelled segment preceding a vowelless identical segment: the elision of one of the identical segments:

In some cases of doubled verbs occurring in the imperative of the 2nd person of the fem pl. in which the vowelled person of the agent, namely the *-na,* is suffixed to, the elision of one the identical segments can be carried out (compare the cases of anomalous perfects in par. 2.2.1.4.).

An example is *ʾiqrir-na* "stay quietly! /2nd person of the fem. pl.", from the root *q r r* with 2nd and 3rd radical r (cf. Ibn Manẓūr, V, 3578-3579), in which the 2nd *r* is vowelless on the basis that the sukūn marks the imperative and that the vowelled agent pronoun is suffixed to it. The sequence of the identical segments in *ʾiqrir-na* is that of a vowelled segment, namely the 2nd radical *r,* preceding a vowelless segment, namely the 3rd radical *r,* which by principle should prevent the assimilation. The elision of the 1st *r* of the sequence is however a possibility after that its vowel is shifted to the *q,* and then the hamza of the imperative is also elided as it is not more needed now that the 1st radical *q* is vowelled. The resulting alleviated form is *qir-na* (cf. Ibn ʿAqīl, II, 584-585, Åkesson, *Ibn Masʿūd* 196: fol. 18b, Penrice, *Dictionary* 116). The variant *qarna* exists as well which pertains to another dialectal variant, and its base form is then the variant *ʾiqrar-na.* It can be mentioned that *wa-qarna* occurs instead of *wa-qirna* in the sur. 33: 33 *(wa-qarna fī buyūtikunna)* and that it is the reading of Nāfiʿ and ʿĀṣim (cf. Ibn ʿAqīl, II, 585).

2.2.1.7. Some derived forms of the verb: the sequence of a vowelled segment preceding a vowelless identical segment: the substitution of one of the doubled segments by a y:

The phonological procedure that is observed in some cases of the derived forms of the doubled verbs is that their 3rd radical, which is the second of two identical segments, is substituted by the *y*.

Sībawaihi, II, 447 mentions the following verbs in which this substitution has been carried out (cf. Roman, *Étude I,* 361):

- Form V *tasarrartu* "I had a concubine" that becomes after the change of the 3rd radical *r* into a *y tasarraytu.*

- Form V *taẓannantu* "I formed an opinion" that becomes after the change of the 3rd radical *n* into a *y taẓannaytu.*

- Form V *taqaṣṣaṣtu* "I remembered [his words]" that becomes after the change of 3rd radical *ṣ* into a *y taqaṣṣaytu.*

- Form IV *ᵓamlaltu* "I dictated" that becomes after the change of 3rd radical l into a *y ᵓamlaytu.*

- Another example that can be added is Form V *taqaḍḍiya* used instead of *taqaḍḍaḍa* "to fly down swiftly" (cf. Zamaḫšarī, 173, Åkesson, *Ibn Masᶜūd* 194: fol. 17b), in which the 3rd radical *ḍ* is changed into the *y,* and the *ḍ* is vowelled with a kasra instead of a fatḥa. The verb is found in the example *taqaḍḍiya l-bāzī* "the hawk flew down swiftly" of the verse said by ᶜAǧǧāǧ cited by Ibn Ǧinnī, *Sirr II,* 759, Muᵓaddib, *Taṣrīf* 438, Ibn Yaᶜīš, X, 24, Åkesson, *Ibn Masᶜūd* 204: (170):

> *"ᵓIḏā l-kirāmu btadarū l-bāᶜa badar*
> *taqaḍḍiya l-bāzī ᵓiḏā l-bāzī kasar".*
> "When the generous hasten to the noble deed,
> he hastens with the swoop of the falcon, when the
> falcon contracts his wings".

3. THE CLASS OF THE HAMZATED VERB

The hamzated verb, *al-mahmūz* is the verb with a hamza radical.

The hamzated verb falls into three classes that refer to the position of the hamza in their forms:

1- verbs with hamza as their 1st radical, e.g. *ʾaḫaḏa* "to take", *ʾakala* "to eat".

2- verbs with hamza as their 2nd radical, e.g. *saʾala* "to ask", *raʾā* "to see".

3- verbs with hamza as their 3rd radical, e.g. *qaraʾa* "to read", *ǧāʾa* "to come".

In this approach of the phonological treatment the focus will be on a few forms in which the two hamzas are combined or in which the hamza is vowelled by a fatḥa and preceded by a vowelless segment.

3.1. The conjugations of the verb with 1st radical hamza

The verb with 1st radical hamza falls into the following conjugations:

1- *faᶜala yafᶜulu,* e.g. *ᵓaḫaḏa yaᵓḫuḏu* "to take".

2- *faᶜala yafᶜilu,* e.g. *ᵓadaba yaᵓdibu* "to invite (to a party or banquet)".

3- *faᶜala yafᶜalu,* e.g. *ᵓahaba yaᵓhabu* "to prepare".

4- *faᶜila yafᶜalu,* e.g. *ᵓariqa yaᵓraqu* "to find no sleep".

5- *faᶜila yafᶜulu,* e.g. *ᵓariğa yaᵓruğu* "to be flagrant".

6- *faᶜala yafᶜulu,* e.g. *ᵓasala yaᵓsulu* "to sharpen".

3.2. Examples of some derivatives and paradigms of the verb with 1st radical hamza

An example of a hamzated verb with 1st radical hamza in the perfect is *ᵓaḫaḏa* "to take". It becomes *yaᵓḫuḏu* in the imperfect of the indicative active. Its imperative is *ḫuḏ,* its active participle is *ʾāḫiḏun,* its *maṣdar* is *ʾaḫḏun,* its perfect passive is *ʾuḫiḏa,* its imperfect is *yuʾḫaḏu* and its passive participle is *maʾḫūḏun.*

Its perfect in the indicative, active, is the following:

	sing.	dual	pl.
1st	*ʾaḫaḏ-tu*		*ʾaḫaḏ-n(a)ā*
2nd masc.	*ʾaḫaḏ-ta*	*ʾaḫaḏ-tum(a)ā*	*ʾaḫaḏ-tum*
2nd fem.	*ʾaḫaḏ-ti*	*ʾaḫaḏ-tum(a)ā*	*ʾaḫaḏ-tunna*
3rd masc.	*ʾaḫaḏa*	*ʾaḫaḏ(a)-ā*	*ʾaḫaḏt(u)-ū*
3rd fem.	*ʾaḫaḏa-t*	*ʾaḫaḏa-t(a)ā*	*ʾaḫaḏ-na*

Its imperfect in the indicative, active, is the following:

	sing.	dual	pl.
1st	*ʾ(a)āḫuḏu*		*naʾḫuḏu*
2nd masc.	*taʾḫuḏu*	*taʾḫuḏ(a)-āni*	*taʾḫuḏ(u)-ūna*
2nd fem.	*taʾḫuḏ(i)-īna*	*taʾḫuḏ(a)-āni*	*taʾḫuḏ-na*
3rd masc.	*yaʾḫuḏu*	*yaʾḫuḏ(a)-āni*	*yaʾḫuḏ(u)-ūna*
3rd fem.	*taʾḫuḏu*	*taʾḫuḏ(a)-āni*	*yaʾḫuḏ-na*

Its imperfect in the indicative, subjunctive, is the following:

	sing.	dual	pl.
1st	*ʾ(a)āḫuḏa*		*naʾḫuḏa*
2nd masc.	*taʾḫuḏa*	*taʾḫuḏ(a)-ā*	*taʾḫuḏ(u)-ū*
2nd fem.	*taʾḫuḏ(i)-ī*	*taʾḫuḏ(a)-ā*	*taʾḫuḏ-na*
3rd masc.	*yaʾḫuḏa*	*yaʾḫuḏ(a)-ā*	*yaʾḫuḏ(u)-ū*
3rd fem.	*taʾḫuḏa*	*taʾḫuḏ(a)-ā*	*yaʾḫuḏ-na*

Its imperfect in the indicative, jussive, is the following:

	sing.	dual	pl.
1st	*ʾ(a)āḫuḏ*		*naʾḫuḏ*
2nd masc.	*taʾḫuḏ*	*taʾḫuḏ(a)-ā*	*taʾḫuḏ(u)-ū*
2nd fem.	*taʾḫuḏ(i)-ī*	*taʾḫuḏ(a)-ā*	*taʾḫuḏ-na*
3rd masc.	*yaʾḫuḏ*	*yaʾḫuḏ(a)-ā*	*yaʾḫuḏ(u)-ū*
3rd fem.	*taʾḫuḏ*	*taʾḫuḏ(a)-ā*	*yaʾḫuḏ-na*

3.2.1. Remarks concerning the phonological procedures in some of its forms:

The verb with 1st radical hamza can present some forms as the imperative and the passive voice in which there occurs a sequence of two hamzas of which the 1st is vowelled and the 2nd is vowelless,

In the case of the imperative, the 1st hamza is the disjunctive hamza of Form I and the 2nd hamza is the 1st radical, e.g. *ʾiʾsir* "capture", and in the case of the passive voice the 1st hamza is the connective hamza of Form IV and the 2nd hamza is the 1st radical of the verb, e.g. *ʾuʾṯira* "he, or it was preferred /(passive)". In both these cases the 2nd vowelless hamza is changed into a glide of the nature of the vowel preceding it.

3.2.1.1. The imperative and the passive voice: the sequence of two hamzas of which the 1st is vowelled and the 2nd is vowelless: the change of the vowelless hamza into a glide:

The forms of verbs with 1st radical hamza that present a combination of two hamzas of which the 1st is vowelled and the 2nd vowelless are the imperative in *ʾifᶜil* of verbs of the conjugation *faᶜala yafᶜilu* and in *ʾufᶜul* of verbs of the conjugation *faᶜala yafᶜulu* and the passive voice of Form IV *ʾufᶜila*.

1- The imperative:

The formation of the imperative in *ʾifᶜil* of verbs with 1st radical hamza of the conjugation *faᶜala yafᶜilu* implies the combination of two hamzas: the vowelled connective hamza of the imperative, the *ʾi,* followed by the vowelless 1st radical hamza of the verb. As the 1st radical hamza of the verb is vowelless, it is subjected to the influence of the connective hamza's vowel, - which is the kasra -, preceding it, and can therefore be changed into a glide of the nature of this vowel, which is the y.

The procedure is the following:

-*ʾiʾ* → -*ʾ(i)y*

An example is *ʾiʾsir* that becomes *ʾiysir* "capture! /2 masc. sing. (imperative)" then *ʾ(i)īsir.*

The formation of the imperative in *ʾufʿul* of verbs with 1st radical hamza of the conjugation *faʿala yafʿulu* results mostly in the elision of both hamzas.

The procedure is then the following:

-*ʾuʾ* → -

Examples are *ḫuḏ* "take!", *kul* "eat!" and *mur* "order!".

The elision of the hamza is obligatory in *ḫuḏ* which is not to be said *ʾuʾḫuḏ* with the combination of both hamzas, or *ʾuwḫuḏ* with the change of the 2nd hamza into a *w* resulting in *ʾu(ū)ḫuḏ,* and in *kul* which is not to be said *ʾuʾkul, ʾuwkul* or *ʾ(u)ūkul.* The elision however is not necessary in *mur* which is allowed, as well as in *ʾuwmur* in which the 1st hamza is maintained and the

1st radical hamza is changed into a *w* resulting in *ʾ(u)ūmur.* Also *ʾamur* with the vowelling of the hamza with a fatḥa occurs as in the sur. 20: 132 *(wa-ʾamur ʾahlaka bi-l-ṣalwati)* "Enjoin prayer on thy people" and in the sur. 7: 199 *(wa-ʾamur bi-l-ᶜurfi ḫuḏi l-ᶜafwa)* "Hold to forgiveness; Command what is right".

<u>*2-The passive voice:*</u>

The formation of the passive voice in Form IV *ʾufᶜila* of verbs with 1st radical hamza implies the combination of the connective hamza, the *ʾu,* and the 1st radical hamza of the verb. The 1st radical hamza, which is vowelless, is subjected to the influence of the ḍamma of the disjunctive hamza preceding it, and is changed into a glide of the nature of this vowel, which is the *w*.

The procedure is the following:

-ʾuʾ → *-ʾ(u)w*

An example is the passive voice of Form IV *ʾuʾṯira* "he, or it was preferred /(passive)", of which the 2nd hamza is changed into a *w,* namely *ʾuwṯira* which then becomes *ʾ(u)ūṯira.*

3.3. The conjugations of the verb with 2nd radical hamza

The verb with 2nd radical hamza falls into the following conjugations:

1- *faᶜala yafᶜalu,* e.g. *saʾala yasʾalu* "to ask". The fatḥa is given to its 2nd radical hamza because the hamza is a guttural consonant in the same manner as it is given to the 2nd radical of the strong verb of which the 2nd or 3rd radical is a guttural consonant.

2- *faᶜila yafᶜalu,* e.g. *yaʾisa yayʾasu* "to despair".

3- *faᶜula yafᶜulu,* e.g. *laʾuma yalʾumu* "to be wicked".

3.4. Examples of some derivatives and paradigms of the verb with 2nd radical hamza

An example of a hamzated verb with 2nd radical hamza in the perfect is *saʾala* "to ask". It becomes *yasʾalu* in the imperfect of the indicative active. Its imperative is *ʾisʾal,* its active participle is *sāʾilun,* its *maṣdar* is *suʾālun,* its perfect passive is *suʾila,* its imperfect is *yusʾalu* and its passive participle is *masʾūlun.*

Its perfect in the indicative, active, is the following:

	sing.	dual	pl.
1st	*saʾal-tu*		*saʾal-n(a)ā*
2nd masc.	*saʾal-ta*	*saʾal-tum(a)ā*	*saʾal-tum*
2nd fem.	*saʾal-ti*	*saʾal-tum(a)ā*	*saʾal-tunna*
3rd masc.	*saʾala*	*saʾal(a)-ā*	*saʾal(u)-ū*
3rd fem.	*saʾala-t*	*saʾala-t(a)ā*	*saʾal-na*

Its imperfect in the indicative, active, is the following:

	sing.	dual	pl.
1st	*ʾasʾalu*		*nasʾalu*
2nd masc.	*tasʾalu*	*tasʾal(a)-āni*	*tasʾal(u)-ūna*
2nd fem.	*tasʾal(i)-īna*	*tasʾal(a)-āni*	*tasʾal-na*
3rd masc.	*yasʾalu*	*yasʾal(a)-āni*	*yasʾal(u)-ūna*
3rd fem.	*tasʾalu*	*tasʾal(a)-āni*	*yasʾal-na*

Its imperfect in the indicative, subjunctive, is the following:

	sing.	dual	pl.
1st	*ʾasʾala*		*nasʾala*
2nd masc.	*tasʾala*	*tasʾal(a)-ā*	*tasʾal(u)-ū*
2nd fem.	*tasʾal(i)-ī*	*tasʾal(a)-ā*	*tasʾal-na*
3rd masc.	*yasʾala*	*yasʾal(a)-ā*	*yasʾal(u)-ū*
3rd fem.	*tasʾala*	*tasʾal(a)-ā*	*yasʾal-na*

Its imperfect in the indicative, jussive, is the following:

	sing.	dual	pl.
1st	*ʾasʾal*		*nasʾal*
2nd masc.	*tasʾal*	*tasʾal(a)-ā*	*tasʾal(u)-ū*
2nd fem.	*tasʾal(i)-ī*	*tasʾal(a)-ā*	*tasʾal-na*
3rd masc.	*yasʾal*	*yasʾal(a)-ā*	*yasʾal(u)-ū*
3rd fem.	*tasʾal*	*tasʾal(a)-ā*	*yasʾal-na*

3.4.1. Remarks concerning the phonological procedures in some of its forms:

The verb with 2nd radical hamza can present some forms as the imperfect (cf. 3.4.1.1.) in which there occurs a sequence of two segments of which the 2nd is a hamza vowelled by a fatḥa and preceded by a vowelless segment. The phonological procedure is that the fatḥa of the hamza is shifted to the vowelless segment preceding it, and the hamza is elided.

3.4.1.1. The imperfect: the sequence of a hamza vowelled by a fatḥa preceded by a sukūn: the transfer of the fatḥa to the vowelless segment and the elision of the hamza:

The 2nd radical hamza is elided by some in the imperfect for the sake of alleviation. Some examples are *yasʾalu* "he asks" that becomes anomalously *yasalu* (cf. de Sacy, I, 236, Wright, II, 77, Vernier, I, 74), and *yarʾ(a)ā* "he sees" that becomes *yar(a)ā* (cf. Sībawaihi, II, 170) on account of the frequency of its usage. It can be remarked that in both *yasʾalu* and *yarʾ(a)ā,* the ʾ is elided and the hamza's fatḥa is shifted to the vowelless segment preceding it. Concerning *yarʾā,* it can be mentioned that in poetry, in consideration to the metric exigency, the ʾ can be retained. This is remarked in *tarʾayāhu* that is used instead of *tarayāhu* in this verse said by Surāqa b. Mirdās al-Azdī al-Bāriqī cited by Ibn Ǧinnī *Sirr I,* 77, II, 826, *Ḫaṣāʾiṣ III,* 153, *de Flexione* 34, Muʾaddib, *Taṣrīf* 422, Ibn Yaʿīš, *Mulūkī* 370, Ibn Manẓūr, III, 1538, Ibn ʿUṣfūr, II, 621, Howell, IV, fasc. I, 941, Åkesson, *Ibn Masʿūd* 266: (236):

"ʾUrī ʿaynayya mā lam tarʾayāhu
kilānā ʿālimun bi-l-turhāti".

"I make my eyes see what they have not seen:
each of us is knowing in falsehoods".

3.5. The conjugations of the hamzated verbs with 3rd radical hamza

The verb with 3rd radical hamza falls into the following conjugations:

1- *faᶜala yafᶜulu,* e.g. *sāʾa yasūʾu* "to become evil".

2- *faᶜala yafᶜilu,* e.g. *ǧāʾa yaǧīʾu* "to come", and *hanaʾa yahniʾu* "to be beneficial".

3- *faᶜala yafᶜalu,* e.g. *našaʾa yanšaʾu* "to emerge", and *sabaʾa yasbaʾu.*

4- *faᶜila yafᶜalu,* e.g. *ṣadiʾa yaṣdaʾu* "to become rusty".

5- *faᶜula yafᶜulu,* e.g. *ǧaruʾa yaǧruʾu* "to dare, venture".

3.6. Examples of some derivatives and paradigms of the hamzated verb with 3rd radical hamza

An example of a hamzated verb with 3rd radical hamza in the perfect is *qaraʾa* "to read". It becomes *yaqraʾu* in the imperfect of the indicative active. Its imperative is *ʾiqraʾ*, its active participle is *qāriʾun,* its *maṣdar* is *qirāʾatun,* its perfect passive is *quriʾa,* its imperfect is *yuqraʾu* and its passive participle is *maqrūʾun.*

Its perfect in the indicative, active, is the following:

	sing.	dual	pl.
1st	*qaraʾ-tu*		*qaraʾ-n(a)ā*
2nd masc.	*qaraʾ-ta*	*qaraʾ-tum(a)ā*	*qaraʾ-tum*
2nd fem.	*qaraʾ-ti*	*qaraʾ-tum(a)ā*	*qaraʾ-tunna*
3rd masc.	*qaraʾa*	*qaraʾ-(a)ā*	*qaraʾ(u)-ū*
3rd fem.	*qaraʾat*	*qaraʾa-t(a)ā*	*qaraʾ-na*

Its imperfect in the indicative, active, is the following:

	sing.	dual	pl.
1st	*ʾaqraʾu*		*naqraʾu*
2nd masc.	*taqraʾu*	*taqraʾ(a)-āni*	*taqraʾ(u)-ūna*
2nd fem.	*taqraʾ(i)-īna*	*taqraʾ(a)-āni*	*taqraʾ-na*
3rd masc.	*yaqraʾu*	*yaqraʾ(a)-āni*	*yaqraʾ(u)-ūna*
3rd fem.	*taqraʾu*	*taqraʾ(a)-āni*	*yaqraʾ-na*

Its imperfect in the indicative, subjunctive, is the following:

	sing.	dual	pl.
1st	*ʾaqraʾa*		*naqraʾa*
2nd masc.	*taqraʾa*	*taqraʾ(a)-ā*	*taqraʾ(u)-ū*
2nd fem.	*taqraʾ(i)-ī*	*taqraʾ(a)-ā*	*taqraʾ-na*
3rd masc.	*yaqraʾa*	*yaqraʾ(a)-ā*	*yaqraʾ(u)-ū*
3rd fem.	*taqraʾa*	*taqraʾ(a)-ā*	*yaqraʾ-na*

Its imperfect in the indicative, jussive, is the following:

	sing.	dual	pl.
1st	*ʾaqraʾ*		*naqraʾ*
2nd masc.	*taqraʾ*	*taqraʾ(a)-ā*	*taqraʾ(u)-ū*
2nd fem.	*taqraʾ(i)-ī*	*taqraʾ(a)-ā*	*taqraʾ-na*
3rd masc.	*yaqraʾ*	*yaqraʾ(a)-ā*	*yaqraʾ(u)-ū*
3rd fem.	*taqraʾ*	*taqraʾ(a)-ā*	*yaqraʾ-na*

3.6.1. Remarks concerning the phonological procedures in some of its forms:

The verb with 3rd radical hamza is treated as the strong verb. The only peculiarity that can be remarked is that the hamza can be dropped in the pronunciation if it it is vowelless and not followed by a suffix (cf. Bakkūš, *Taṣrīf* 118, ᶜAbd al-Raḥīm, *Ṣarf* 26-27). Hence *lam yaqraʾ* "he did not read" can be pronounced *lam yaqra.*

3.7. The occurrence of the hamza in some of the other classes of irregular verbs

The hamza can occur as a radical in other classes of verbs than the "purely" hamzated. The following cases can be mentioned:

1- as a 1st radical in the doubled verb, e.g. *ʾanna yaʾinnu* "to groan, moan".

2- as a 2nd radical in verbs with weak 1st radical, e.g. *waʾada* "to bury alive (a newborn girl)", and as a 3rd radical in a verb with weak 1st radical, e.g. *waǧaʾa* "to beat".

3- as a 1st or 3rd radical in verbs with weak 2nd radical, e.g. *ʾāna* "to come, to approach" and *ǧāʾa* "to come" respectively.

4- as a 1st or 2nd radical in verbs with weak 3rd radical, e.g. *ʾabā* [with final *alif maqṣūra]* "to refuse" and *raʾā* [with final *alif maqṣūra]* "to see" respectively.

5- as a 2nd radical in verbs with weak 1st and 3rd radical, e.g. *waʾā* [with final *alif maqṣūra]* "to promise".

6- as a 1st radical in verbs with 2nd and 3rd weak radical, e.g. *ʾawā* [with final *alif maqṣūra]* "to seek refuge".

4. THE CLASS OF THE VERB WITH 1ST RADICAL W OR Y

The verb with 1st *w* or y radical is generally termed as *muᶜtal al-fāʾ*.

Another nomination is *miṯālun* "assimilated, similar", which is given to it because some of its patterns are similar to other patterns of verb classes.

This similarity is noticed in two cases:

1- Its pattern of the perfect that is formed of three radicals is similar to the pattern of the perfect of the strong verb, as its 1st weak radical is retained and sound as is the 1st strong radical of the strong verb. This can be illustrated with the following example:

<u>*a- verb with 1st radical w*</u>

wa^{c}ada "to promise"		*ḍaraba* "to hit"
1st sound *w* radical	=	1st strong radical
wa+^{c}a+da		*ḍa+ra+ba*
1 + 2 + 3 radicals		1 + 2 + 3 radicals

<u>*b- verb with 1st radical y*</u>

yasara "to play at hasard"		*ḍaraba* "to hit"
1st sound *y* radical	=	1st strong radical
ya+sa+ra		*ḍa+ra+ba*
1 + 2 + 3 radicals		1 + 2 + 3 radicals

2 - Its pattern of the imperative that is formed of two radicals is similar to the pattern of the imperative of the verb with 2nd *w* or *y* radical. This can be illustrated with the following example:

^{c}*id* "promise!"		*zin* "decorate"
(from *wa^{c}ada)*		(from *zayana)*
elision of 1st radical *w*	=	elision of 2nd radical *y*
^{c}*i+d*		*zi+n*
1 + 2 radicals		1 + 2 radicals

The imperative of the verb with 1st radical *w:* ^{c}*id* is underlyingly ^{ɔ}*iw^{c}id* formed according to the measure ^{ɔ}*if^{c}il* (from *wa^{c}ada)* with the 1st radical *w* elided and the imperative of the verb with 2nd *y* radical *zin* is underlyingly ^{ɔ}*izyin* formed according to ^{ɔ}*if^{c}il* (from *zayana)* with the 2nd *y* radical elided.

4.1. The conjugations of the verb with 1st radical *w*

The conjugations of the verb with 1st radical *w* can conveniently be grouped into the following ones:

1- *fa^{c}ala yaf^{c}ilu,* e.g. *wa^{c}ada yaw^{c}idu* "to promise", of which the imperfect *yaw^{c}idu* becomes after the phonological change *ya^{c}idu* with the 1st radical *w* elided.

2- *fa^cala yaf^calu,* e.g. *wahaba yawhabu* "to give", of which the imperfect *yawhabu* becomes after the phonological change *yahabu* with the 1st radical *w* elided.

3- *fa^cila yaf^calu,* e.g. *wağila yawğalu* "to be afraid", of which the 1st radical *w* is maintained in the imperfect *yawğalu.*

4- *fa^cila yaf^cilu,* e.g. *wamiqa yawmiqu* "to love", of which the imperfect *yawmiqu* becomes after the phonological change *yamiqu* with the 1st radical *w* elided.

5- *fa^cula yaf^culu,* e.g. *wabula yawbulu* "to be unwholesome", of which the 1st radical *w* is maintained in the imperfect *yawbulu.*

4.1.1. An anomalous case: wağada yağudu

An anomalous case is the verb *wağada yağudu* "to find, to experience" in which the theme vowel is a ḍamma, and which would seem to be formed according to the conjugation *fa^cala yaf^culu.* However a deeper level of analysis shows that its theme vowel is a kasra, as the underlying conjugation is *wağada yağidu* formed according to the conjugation *fa^cala yaf^cilu.* The imperfect *yağidu* is underlyingly *yawğidu* of which the 1st radical *w* is elided and the 2nd radical, the *ğ,* is given the kasra, namely *yağidu.* This procedure occurs by all the Arabs except by the Banū ^cĀmir (cf. Ibn Manẓūr, VI, 4769, Åkesson, *Ibn*

Mas^cūd 270: fol. 25b) who give the *ǧ* the ḍamma, namely *yaǧudu.* The example of the imperfect of the 3rd person of the fem. pl. *yaǧudna* that occurs in their dialect in this verse said by Ǧarīr, cited by Ibn [c]Uṣfūr, I, 177, Ibn Ya[c]īš, *Mulūkī* 49, Howell, II-III, 247-248, Åkesson, *Ibn Mas[c]ūd* 274: (243) can be mentioned:

> *"Law šiʾti qad naqaʿa l-fuʾāda bi-šarbatin*
> *tadaʿu l-ṣawādiya lā yaǧudna ġalīlan".*
> "If you had wanted, your saliva would have quenched [the thirst] of the heart with a single draught
> leaving the thirsty [ribs of the breast in such a state that] they would not experience heat of thirst".

4.2. Examples of some derivatives and paradigms of the verb with 1st radical *w*

An example of a verb with 1st radical *w* in the perfect is *waʿada* "to promise". It becomes *yaʿidu* in the imperfect of the indicative active. Its imperative is *ʿid,* its active participle is *wāʿidun,* its *maṣdar* is *waʿdun* or *ʿidatun,* its perfect passive is *wuʿida,* its imperfect is *yūʿadu* and its passive participle is *mawʿūdun.*

Its paradigm in the perfect, active, is as follows:

	sing.	dual	pl.
1st	waᶜad-tu		waᶜad-n(a)ā
2nd masc.	waᶜad-ta	waᶜad-tum(a)ā	waᶜad-tum
2nd fem.	waᶜad-ti	waᶜad-tum(a)ā	waᶜad-tunna
3rd masc.	waᶜada	waᶜad(a)-ā	waᶜad(u)-ū
3rd fem.	waᶜada-t	waᶜada-t(a)ā	waᶜad-na

Its imperfect in the indicative, active, is the following:

	sing.	dual	pl.
1st	ʾaᶜidu		naᶜidu
2nd masc.	taᶜidu	taᶜid(a)-āni	taᶜid(u)-ūna
2nd fem.	taᶜid(i)-īna	taᶜid(a)-āni	taᶜid-na
3rd masc.	yaᶜidu	yaᶜid(a)-āni	yaᶜid(u)-ūna
3rd fem.	taᶜidu	taᶜid(a)-āni	yaᶜid-na

Its imperfect in the indicative, subjunctive, is the following:

	sing.	dual	pl.
1st	ʾaᶜida		naᶜida
2nd masc.	taᶜida	taᶜid(a)-ā	taᶜid(u)-ū
2nd fem.	taᶜid(i)-ī	taᶜid(a)-ā	taᶜid-na
3rd masc.	yaᶜida	yaᶜid(a)-ā	yaᶜid(u)-ū
3rd fem.	taᶜida	taᶜid(a)-ā	yaᶜid-na

Its imperfect in the indicative, jussive, is the following:

	sing.	dual	pl.
1st	*ʾaᶜid*		*naᶜid*
2nd masc.	*taᶜid*	*taᶜid(a)-ā*	*taᶜid(u)-ū*
2nd fem.	*taᶜid(i)-ī*	*taᶜid(a)-ā*	*taᶜid-na*
3rd masc.	*yaᶜid*	*yaᶜid(a)-ā*	*yaᶜid(u)-ū*
3rd fem.	*taᶜid*	*taᶜid(a)-ā*	*yaᶜid-na*

4.2.1. Remarks concerning the phonological procedures in some of its forms:

The main phonological changes are that it can have in some of its forms its 1st radical sound, in others elided and in others changed into another segment.

A few different forms with various sequences are presented here with the aim of determining some main phonological rules.

4.2.1.1. The perfect: the sequence in which the 1st radical *w* is the initial segment: the soundness of the glide.

4.2.1.2. The verbal noun: the sequence in which the 1st radical *w* is the initial segment: the elision of the *w* and the compensation with the prefixed *tāʾ marbūṭā*.

4.2.1.3. The imperfect: the sequence in which the 1st radical *w* is vowelless and followed by a kasra in the conjugation *yafᶜilu:* the elision of the *w*.

4.2.1.4. The imperfect: the sequence in which the 1st radical *w* is vowelless and followed by a fatḥa in the conjugation *yafᶜalu:* the retaining or the change of the *w* into a *y* or an *ā*, or the elision of the *w*.

4.2.1.5. The imperative: the sequence in which the 1st radical *w* is vowelless and preceded by the kasra of the connective hamza: the *w* is changed into a *y* and can be retained or is elided together with the hamza vowelled by a kasra.

4.2.1.6. The active participle: the sequence in which the 1st radical *w* is vowelled by a fatḥa and followed by the infix vowelless *ā:* the retaining of the *w* or the anomalous transposition of segments.

4.2.1.7. The noun of place and time: the sequence in which the 1st radical *w* is vowelless and preceded by a fatḥa: the soundness of the *w*.

4.2.1.8. Form VIII of the perfect: the sequence in which the 1st vowelless radical *w* is preceded by a kasra and followed by the vowelled infixed *t:* the change of the *w* into a *y* and the assimilation of the *y* to the vowelled infixed *t*.

4.2.1.1. The perfect: the sequence in which the 1st radical w is the initial segment: the soundness of the glide:

The 1st weak radical remains sound in the perfect, e.g. *wa*ᶜ*ada* "he promised" on the basis that the glide can only be affected by a phonological change if it is preceded by another segment, which is not the case here as the glide is the initial segment.

This rule implies that no phonological change can affect the initial segment. Hence, this means that the *w* in *wa*ᶜ*ada* cannot be made vowelless resulting in *w*ᶜ*ada,* because of the impossibility of beginning the word with a vowelless segment. It could not either be changed into *ā* resulting in *ā*ᶜ*ada* as this would imply beginning the word with a vowelless segment which is forbidden, and it could not either be elided as the root would seem to be formed of two radicals, i.e. ᶜ*ada,* which is not allowed (cf. Åkesson, *Ibn Mas*ᶜ*ūd* 270: fol. 25b-26a).

*4.2.1.2. The verbal noun: the sequence in which the 1st radical w is the initial segment: the elision of the w and the compensation with the prefixed tā*ʾ *marbūṭā:*

It can be stated that the 1st weak radical can be elided in some cases of verbal nouns, e.g. ᶜ*idatun* underlyingly *wi*ᶜ*dun* "a promise" (for some examples see Suyūṭī, *Muẓhir II,* 158-159), in spite of the fact that it is the initial segment of the word. This opposes the rule that the glide should be preceded by another segment if a phonological change is to be carried out. The breaking of this rule requests however that the *tāʾ marbūṭa* is suffixed to it as a compensation for the elision of this initial glide (cf. Sībawaihi, II, 81, Wright, II, 118, Lane, II, 2952).

Not only the *tāʾ marbūṭa* can occur as a compensation of a glide in the same word, but also another word, occurring as the 2nd element of an *ʾiḍāfa* construction, can occur as a compensation for the elision of a *tāʾ marbūṭa.* An eample is the case of the *tāʾ marbūṭa* that is anomalously elided from the accusative *ᶜidata* which is said *ᶜida,* when it occurs as the first element of a construct state in this verse said by Abū Umayya al-Faḍl b. al-ᶜAbbās b. ᶜUtba b. Abī Lahab, that is cited by Ibn Ǧinnī, *Ḫaṣāʾiṣ III,* 171, Muʾaddib, *Taṣrīf* 285, Suyūṭī, *Ašbāh III,* 248, Ibn Manẓūr, VI, 4871, Howell, I, fasc. IV, 1527-1528, IV, fasc. I, 1423-1424, Åkesson, *Ibn Masᶜūd* 277: (248):

"ʾInna l-ḫalīṭa ʾaǧaddū l-bayna fa-nǧaradū
wa-ʾaḫlafūka ᶜida l-ʾamri l-laḏī waᶜadū".
"Verily the familiar friends have renewed the
separation, and made off, and have broken to you
the promise of the matter which they promised".

There exist two different theories concerning the elision of the *tāʾ marbūṭa* from *ᶜidatun* and its likes. One of them is Sībawaihi's theory (cf. Sībawaihi, II, 260-261) who accepts the elision of the *tāʾ marbūṭa* even when the word to which it is suffixed to is not the first element of a construct state, and the other one is al-Farrāʾs, who can only accept this elision when the word is the first element of the construct state, as in the case of *ᶜida l-ʾamri* of this verse, as he considers the second element of the construct, namely *l-ʾamri,* as a compensation for the elided *tāʾ marbūṭa* (cf. Muʾaddib, *Taṣrīf* 285, Åkesson, *Ibn Masᶜūd* 270-272: fol. 26a).

4.2.1.3. The imperfect: the sequence in which the 1st radical w is vowelless and followed by a kasra in the conjugation yafᶜilu: the elision of the w:

In some examples of verbs occurring in the imperfect formed according to *yafᶜilu,* e.g. *yawᶜidu* "he promises", the *w* is elided as it precedes a kasra, which is deemed as a heavy combination resulting in *yaᶜidu* (cf. Zamaḫšarī, 178, de Sacy, I, 238, Vernier, I, 57).

The Kufans believed that the elision of the *w* is to distinguish the transitive verbs, e.g. *yaᶜidu-hu* underlyingly *yawᶜidu-hu* "he promises him/it", *yazinu-hu* underlyingly *yawzinu-hu* "he weights him/it", from the intransitive verbs in which the *w* is retained, e.g. *yawḥalu* "he/it falls into the mud", and *yawǧalu* "he fears". Their theory is however vicious as there exist verbs in the intransitive in which the *w* is elided, e.g. *yakifu* said with the elision of the *w* instead of *yawkifu* "it drips with rain-water" (for discussions see Ibn al-Anbārī, *Inṣāf* Q. 112, 326-327, Howell, IV, fasc. I, 1418).

4.2.1.4. The imperfect: the sequence in which the 1st radical w is vowelless and followed by a fatḥa in the conjugation yafᶜalu: the retaining or the change of the w into a y or an ā, or the elision of the w:

The *w* is usually maintained in the imperfect of the conjugation *faᶜila yafᶜalu,* e.g. *wağila yawğalu* "to be afraid". In some rare cases it is changed into a *y,* namely *wağila yawğalu* or *yayğalu, wağiᶜa yawğaᶜu* or *yayğaᶜu* "to have pain", and in some more rare cases into an *ā,* namely *y(a)āğalu* and *y(a)āgaᶜu* (cf. Wright, II, 79, Bakkūš, *Taṣrīf* 125).

The *w* is elided in the imperfect of the conjugation *faᶜala yafᶜalu,* e.g. *wahaba yahabu* "to give" underlyingly *wahaba yawhabu.*

As for the reason why the *w* is maintained in the conjugation *faᶜila yafᶜalu* and elided in *faᶜala yafᶜalu,* it seems to be to distinguish both these conjugations from each other (cf. Bakkūš, *Taṣrīf* 125, ᶜAbd al-Raḥīm, *Ṣarf* 28-29).

4.2.1.5. The imperative: the sequence in which the 1st radical w is vowelless and preceded by the kasra of the connective hamza: the w is changed into a y and can be retained or is elided together with the hamza vowelled by a kasra:

In the case of the imperative that is formed according to *ʾifᶜal,* e.g. *ʾiwǧal,* the *w* is vowelless and preceded by the kasra of the connective hamza. The *w* is changed into a *y,* namely *ʾiyǧal* "be scared!" on account of the influence of the kasra (cf. Wright, II, 80).

In the case of *ʾifᶜil,* e.g. *ʾiwᶜid* "promise /masc sing.", the vowelless *w* is at first changed into a *y* on account of the kasra preceding it, namely *ʾiyᶜid* (cf. Wright, II, 78, de Sacy, I, 238), then both the hamza vowelled by a kasra, namely the *ʾi,* and the *y* are elided resulting in *ᶜid.* This elision of the 1st radical *w* changed into *y* seems to be on the analogy of its elision in the imperfect (for it see par. 4.2.1.3.) *taᶜidu,* as the imperative can be considered to be derived from the imperfect.

4.2.1.6. The active participle: the sequence in which the 1st radical w is vowelled by a fatḥa and followed by the infix vowelless ā: the retaining of the w or the anomalous transposition of segments:

The active participle's form is *f(a)āᶜilun,* e.g. *w(a)āᶜidun* "promising", in which the *w* is sound.

In some anomalous cases the *qalb* "transfer of one segment to the position of another one" is carried out (for an example concerning the active participle of a verb with 2nd *w* radical, e.g. *š(a)āwikun* > *š(a)ākin* see par. 5.5.10.: 2).

An example is *w(a)āḥidun* "one (in higher ordinals)" resulting in *ḥ(a)ādin* (cf. Åkesson, *Ibn Masᶜūd* 292: fol. 30b). An analysis of the phonological changes that are carried out in it shows us that the 1st radical *w* is shifted after the 3rd radical *d* resulting in *āḥidwun.* As it is impossible to start the word with a vowelless *ā,* the 2nd radical *ḥ* is shifted before it and the kasra of the *ḥ* is shifted after the vowelless *d,* so that it became *ḥ(a)ādiwun.* The *w* in *ḥ(a)ādiwun* is changed into a *y* on account of the kasra preceding it, so it became *ḥ(a)ādiyun.* As it resembles the active participles of verbs with 3rd weak radical, e.g. *r(a)āmiyun* "The one who throws" that becomes *r(a)āmin* in both the nominative and the genitive (cf. 6.5.12 and compare the case of the active participle of the verb with 2nd radical *š(a)ākin* par. 5.5.10.: 2), a phonological change was carried out in it so that it became *ḥ(a)ādin.* So the pattern of *ḥ(a)ādin* is not *fāᶜilun* but *ᶜālifun* (cf. Ibn Manẓūr, VI, 4779).

4.2.1.7. The noun of place and time: the sequence in which the 1st radical w is vowelless and preceded by a fatḥa: the soundness of the w:

The form of the noun of place and time of the verb with 1st radical *w* is *mafᶜilun.* The 1st radical *w* is retained in it and the

2nd radical is invariably vowelled with a kasra. Examples are *mawᶜidun* "time or place of a promise or appointment" from *waᶜada yaᶜidu* "to promise" of the conjugation *faᶜala yafᶜilu* and *mawǧilun* "a place that is dreaded" from *waǧila yawǧalu* "to be afraid" of the conjugation *faᶜila yafᶜalu.*

4.2.1.8. Form VIII of the perfect: the sequence in which the 1st vowelless radical w is preceded by a kasra and followed by the vowelled infixed t: the change of the w into a y and the assimilation of the y to the vowelled infixed t:

In the Form VIII of the perfect *ᵓiftaᶜala,* e.g. *ᵓiwtaᶜada* "to accept a promise", the *w* is changed into a *y* on account of the kasra of the connective hamza preceding it, namely *ᵓiytaᶜada,* and the *y* is assimilated to the infixed *t,* resulting in *ᵓittaᶜada.*

4.3. The conjugations of the verb with 1st radical *y*

The conjugations of the verb with 1st radical *y* can conveniently be grouped into the following ones:

1- *faᶜala yafᶜilu,* e.g. *yasara yaysiru* “to be easy” and *yanaᶜa yayniᶜu* "to become ripe", of which the imperfect is inflected as the strong verb, namely *yayniᶜu* or *yaynaᶜu.*

2- *faᶜala yafᶜalu,* e.g. *yafaᶜa yayfaᶜu* "to be grown up", of which the imperfect is inflected as the strong verb, namely *yayfaᶜu.*

3- *faᶜila yafᶜalu,* e.g. *yaqiẓa yayqaẓu* "to be awake", of which the imperfect is inflected as the strong verb, namely *yayqaẓu.*

4- *faᶜula yafᶜulu,* e.g. *yaquẓa yayquẓu* "to be awake", of which the imperfect is inflected as the strong verb, namely *yayquẓu.*

4.4. Examples of some derivatives and paradigms of the verb with 1st radical *y*

An example of a verb with 1st radical *y* in the perfect is *yasara* "to be easy". It becomes *yaysiru* in the imperfect of the indicative active. Its imperative is *ᵓiysir* > *ᵓīsir,* its active participle is *yāsirun,* its *maṣdar* is *yasrun,* its passive is *yusira,* its imperfect is *yūsaru* and its passive participle is *maysūrun.*

Its paradigm in the perfect, active, is as follows:

	sing.	dual	pl.
1st	*yasar-tu*		*yasar-n(a)ā*
2nd masc.	*yasar-ta*	*yasar-tum(a)ā*	*yasar-tum*
2nd fem.	*yasar-ti*	*yasar-tum(a)ā*	*yasar-tunna*
3rd masc.	*yasara*	*yasar(a)-ā*	*yasar(u)-ū*
3rd fem.	*yasara-t*	*yasara-t(a)ā*	*yasar-na*

Its imperfect in the indicative, active, is the following:

	sing.	dual	pl.
1st	*ʾaysiru*		*naysiru*
2nd masc.	*taysiru*	*taysir(a)-āni*	*taysir(u)-ūna*
2nd fem.	*taysir(i)-īna*	*taysir(a)-āni*	*taysir-na*
3rd masc.	*yaysiru*	*yaysir(a)-āni*	*yaysir(u)-ūna*
3rd fem.	*taysiru*	*taysir(a)-āni*	*yaysir-na*

Its imperfect in the indicative, subjunctive, is the following:

	sing.	dual	pl.
1st	*ʾaysira*		*naysira*
2nd masc.	*taysira*	*taysir(a)-ā*	*taysir(u)-ū*
2nd fem.	*taysir(i)-ī*	*taysir(a)-ā*	*taysir-na*
3rd masc.	*yaysira*	*yaysir(a)-ā*	*yaysir(u)-ū*
3rd fem.	*taysira*	*taysir(a)-ā*	*yaysir-na*

Its imperfect in the indicative, jussive, is the following:

	sing.	dual	pl.
1st	*ᵓaysir*		*naysir*
2nd masc.	*taysir*	*taysir(a)-ā*	*taysir(u)-ū*
2nd fem.	*taysir(i)-ī*	*taysir(a)-ā*	*taysir-na*
3rd masc.	*yaysir*	*yaysir(a)-ā*	*yaysir(u)-ū*
3rd fem.	*taysir*	*taysir(a)-ā*	*yaysir-na*

4.4.1. Some remarks concerning the phonological procedures in some of its forms:

It is possible to observe that the verb with 1st radical *y* has in most forms the *y* retained. However the *y* is changed into a *w* when it occurs vowelless and preceded by a ḍamma.

The procedure is then the following:

-uy → *-uw > (u)ū*

The forms that present such a sequence are the imperfect of the passive voice of Form I *yufᶜalu,* the active voice of Form IV of the imperfect *yufᶜilu* and the active participle of Form IV *mufᶜilun.* The following forms shall be considered in order to be able to determine the main rules concerning the various sequences in them:

4.4.1.1. The imperfect of the passive voice of Form I, the active voice of Form IV of the imperfect and the active participle of Form IV: the *y* is vowelless and preceded by a ḍamma: the change of the *y* into a *w*.

4.4.1.2. Form VIII of the perfect: the sequence in which the 1st vowelless radical *y* is preceded by a kasra and followed by the vowelled infixed *t:* the assimilation of the *y* to the vowelled infixed *t.*

4.4.1.1. The imperfect of the passive voice of Form I, the active voice of Form IV of the imperfect and the active participle of Form IV: the y is vowelless and preceded by a ḍamma: the change of the y into a w:

An example of an imperfect of the passive voice of Form I *yufᶜalu,* is *yuysaru* that becomes *yuwsaru* > *y(u)ūsaru* "is pleased".

The same change of the *y* into *w* is carried out in the active voice of Form IV of the imperfect *yuysiru* that becomes *yuwsiru* > *y(u)ūsiru* "is well off" (cf. Wright, II, 50). Thus *yuysiru* with the vowelless *y* preceded by a ḍamma becomes *yuwsiru* with the *y* changed into a *w.* As *yuwsiru* has its vowelless *w* preceded by a ḍamma, it becomes *y(u)ūsiru* with the *w* changed into an *ū.*

The same applies for the active participle Form IV *muysirun* that becomes *muwsirun* > *m(u)ūsirun* "is prosperous" (cf. Åkesson, *Ibn Mas^cūd* 286: fol. 28a-28b). Thus *muysirun* with the vowelless 1st radical *y* preceded by a ḍamma becomes *muwsirun* with the *y* changed into a *w*. As *muwsirun* has its vowelless *w* preceded by a ḍamma it becomes *m(u)ūsirun* with the *w* changed into an *ū*. The reason of the change of the vowelless *y* into a *w* is the influence of the ḍamma of the segment preceding the *y* and the faintness of the nature of the vowelless segment in relation to the vowelled segment.

4.4.1.2. Form VIII of the perfect: the sequence in which the 1st vowelless radical y is preceded by a kasra and followed by the vowelled infixed t: the assimilation of the y to the vowelled infixed t:

In the Form VIII of the perfect *ᵓifta^cala,* e.g. *ᵓiytasara* "to play at hazard", the *y* is assimilated to the infixed *t,* resulting in *ᵓittasara.*

5. THE CLASS OF THE VERB WITH 2ND RADICAL W OR Y

The verb with 2nd radical *w* or *y, al-mu*ᶜ*tall al-*ᶜ*ayn,* is also termed *al-*ᵓ*ağwaf* "the hollow verb". Another less known nomination is *ḏū l-ṯalāṯat* "the one with three segments" (cf. Åkesson, *Ibn Mas*ᶜ*ūd* 282: fol. 26b), which is given to it because it loses its 2nd weak radical in the perfect when the vowelled suffixed agent pronoun, namely the *-tu* "/1st person of the sing.", *-ta* "2nd person of the masc. sing.", *-ti* "2nd person of the fem. sing.", *-tumā* "2nd person of the dual", *-tum* "2nd person of the masc. pl.", *-tunna* "2nd person of the fem. pl.", or *-na* "3rd person of the fem pl., is attached to it. It comprehends three segments instead of four in these perfect forms, which distinguishes it from the other classes of verbs. This can be illustrated with the following examples:

a- verb with 2nd radical w

An example of a verb with 2nd radical *w* is *qul-tu* "I said" underlyingly *qawal-tu* (for the phonological change see 5.5.2.1.: 1) that loses the *w* radical, and hence *qul-ta* "you said /masc. sing." underlyingly *qawal-ta, qul-ti* "you said /fem. sing." underlyingly *qawal-ti, qul-tumā* "you said /dual" underlyingly *qawal-tumā, qul-tum* "you said /dual." underlyingly *qawal-tum, qawal-na* "they said /fem. pl." underlyingly *qawal-na,* etc.

The underlying form that comprehends four segments can be distinguished from the form in which a phonological change due to the unsound glide is carried out, resulting in three segments. This can be illustrated as follows:

The underlying form is:

qawal-tu	=	*fa*^{c}*al-tu*
qa+wa+l+tu	=	*fa+*^{c}*a+l+tu*
1 + 2 + 3 + 4 segments	=	1 + 2 + 3 + 4 segments

The form in which a phonological change is carried out is:

qu+l+tu	=	*fu+l+tu*
1 + 2 + 3 segments	=	1 + 2 + 3 segments

<u>*b- verb with 2nd radical y*</u>

An example of a verb with 2nd radical *y* is *bi^c-tu* "I sold" underlyingly *baya^c-tu* (for the phonological change see par. 5.5.1.2.: 1) that loses the *y* radical, and hence *bi^c-ta* "you said /masc. sing." underlyingly *baya^c-ta*, *bi^c-ti* "you said /fem. sing." underlyingly *baya^c-ti*, *bi^c-na* "they said /fem. pl." underlyingly *baya^c-na*, etc.

The underlying form is:

baya^c-tu	=	*fa^{c}al-tu*
ba+ya+^{c}+tu	=	*fa+^{c}a+l+tu*
1 + 2 + 3 + 4 segments	=	1 + 2 + 3 + 4 segments

The form in which a phonological change is carried out:

bi+^{c}+tu	=	*fi+l+tu*
1 + 2 + 3 segments	=	1 + 2 + 3 segments

5.1. The conjugations of the verb with 2nd radical *w*

The conjugations of the verb with 2nd radical *w* can be grouped into the following:

1- *fa^c^ala yaf^c^ulu,* e.g. *qawala yaqwulu* that becomes after the phonological change *qāla yaqūlu* "to say".

2- *fa^c^ila yaf^c^alu,* e.g. *ḫawifa yaḫwafu* that becomes after the phonological change *ḫāfa yaḫāfu* "to fear".

3- *fa^c^ula yaf^c^ulu,* e.g. *ṭawula yaṭwulu* that becomes after the phonological change *ṭāla yaṭūlu* "to become long".

5.2. Examples of some derivatives and paradigms of the verb with 2nd radical *w*

An example of a verb with 2nd radical *w* in the perfect is *qāla* "to ask". It becomes *yaqūlu* in the imperfect of the indicative active. Its imperative is *qul,* its active participle is *qā^ʾ^ilun,* its *maṣdar* is *qawlun,* its perfect passive is *qīla,* its imperfect is *yuqālu* and its passive participle is *maqūlun.*

Its paradigm in the perfect, active, is as follows:

	sing.	dual	pl.
1st	*qul-tu*		*qul-n(a)ā*
2nd masc.	*qul-ta*	*qul-tum(a)ā*	*qul-tum*
2nd fem.	*qul-ti*	*qul-tum(a)ā*	*qul-tunna*
3rd masc.	*q(a)āla*	*q(a)āl(a)-ā*	*q(a)āl(u)-ū*
3rd fem.	*q(a)āla-t*	*q(a)āla-t(a)ā*	*qul-na*

Its imperfect in the indicative, active, is the following:

	sing.	dual	pl.
1st	*ʾaq(u)ūlu*		*naq(u)ūlu*
2nd masc.	*taq(u)ūlu*	*taq(u)ūl(a)-āni*	*taq(u)ūl(u)-ūna*
2nd fem.	*taq(u)ūl(i)-īna*	*taq(u)ūl(a)-āni*	*taqul-na*
3rd masc.	*yaq(u)ūlu*	*yaq(u)ūl(a)-āni*	*yaq(u)ūl(u)-ūna*
3rd fem.	*taq(u)ūlu*	*taq(u)ūl(a)-āni*	*yaqul-na*

Its imperfect in the indicative, subjunctive, is the following:

	sing.	dual	pl.
1st	*ʾaq(u)ūla*		*naq(u)ūla*
2nd masc.	*taq(u)ūla*	*taq(u)ūl(a)-ā*	*taq(u)ūl(u)-ū*
2nd fem.	*taq(u)ūl(i)-ī*	*taq(u)ūl(a)-ā*	*taqul-na*
3rd masc.	*yaq(u)ūla*	*yaq(u)ūl(a)-ā*	*yaq(u)ūl(u)-ū*
3rd fem.	*taq(u)ūla*	*taq(u)ūl(a)-ā*	*yaqul-na*

Its imperfect in the indicative, jussive, is the following:

	sing.	dual	pl.
1st	*ᵓaqul*		*naqul*
2nd masc.	*taqul*	*taq(u)ūl(a)-ā*	*taq(u)ūl(u)-ū*
2nd fem.	*taq(u)ūl(i)-ī*	*taq(u)ūl(a)-ā*	*taqul-na*
3rd masc.	*yaqul*	*yaq(u)ūl(a)-ā*	*yaq(u)ūl(u)-ū*
3rd fem.	*taqul*	*taq(u)ūl(a)-ā*	*yaqul-na*

5.3. The conjugations of the verb with 2nd radical *y*

The conjugations of the verb with 2nd radical *y* can be grouped into the following:

1- *faᶜala yafᶜilu,* e.g. *bayaᶜa yabyiᶜu* that becomes after the phonological change *bāᶜa yabīᶜu* "to sell".

2- *faᶜila yafᶜalu,* e.g. *hayiba yahyabu* that becomes after the phonological change *hāba yahābu* "to fear".

5.4. Examples of some derivatives and paradigms of the verb with 2nd radical *y:*

An example of a verb with 2nd radical *y* in the perfect is *bāᶜa* "to buy". It becomes *yabīᶜu* in the imperfect of the indicative active. Its imperative is *biᶜ*, its active participle is *bāʾiᶜun,* its *maṣdar* is *bayᶜun,* its perfect passive is *bīᶜa,* its imperfect is *yubāᶜu* and its passive participle is *mabīᶜun.*

Its paradigm in the perfect, active, is as follows:

	sing.	dual	pl.
1st	*biᶜ-tu*		*biᶜ-n(a)ā*
2nd masc.	*biᶜ-ta*	*biᶜ-tum(a)ā*	*biᶜ-tum*
2nd fem.	*biᶜ-ti*	*biᶜ-tum(a)ā*	*biᶜ-tunna*
3rd masc.	*b(a)āᶜa*	*b(a)āᶜ(a)-ā*	*b(a)āᶜ(u)-ū*
3rd fem.	*b(a)āᶜa-t*	*b(a)āᶜa-t(a)ā*	*biᶜ-na*

Its imperfect in the indicative, active, is the following:

	sing.	dual	pl.
1st	*ʾab(i)īᶜu*		*nab(i)īᶜu*
2nd masc.	*tab(i)īᶜu*	*tab(i)īᶜ(a)-āni*	*tab(i)īᶜ(u)-ūna*
2nd fem.	*tab(i)īᶜ(i)-īna*	*tab(i)īᶜ(a)-āni*	*tabiᶜ-na*
3rd masc.	*yab(i)īᶜu*	*yab(i)īᶜ(a)-āni*	*yab(i)īᶜ(u)-ūna*
3rd fem.	*tab(i)īᶜu*	*tab(i)īᶜ(a)-āni*	*yabiᶜ-na*

Its imperfect in the indicative, subjunctive, is the following:

	sing.	dual	pl.
1st	*ʾab(i)ī^c^a*		*nab(i)ī^c^a*
2nd masc.	*tab(i)ī^c^a*	*tab(i)ī^c^(a)-ā*	*tab(i)ī^c^(u)-ū*
2nd fem.	*tab(i)ī^c^(i)-ī*	*tab(i)ī^c^(a)-ā*	*tabi^c^-na*
3rd masc.	*yab(i)ī^c^a*	*yab(i)ī^c^(a)-ā*	*yab(i)ī^c^(u)-ū*
3rd fem.	*tab(i)ī^c^a*	*tab(i)ī^c^(a)-ā*	*yabi^c^-na*

Its imperfect in the indicative, jussive, is the following:

	sing.	dual	pl.
1st	*ʾabi^c^*		*nabi^c^*
2nd masc.	*tabi^c^*	*tab(i)ī^c^(a)-ā*	*tab(i)ī^c^(u)-ū*
2nd fem.	*tab(i)ī^c^(i)-ī*	*tab(i)ī^c^(a)-ā*	*tabi^c^-na*
3rd masc.	*yabi^c^*	*yab(i)ī^c^(a)-ā*	*yab(i)ī^c^(u)-ū*
3rd fem.	*tabi^c^*	*tab(i)ī^c^(a)-ā*	*yabi^c^-na*

5.5. Remarks concerning the phonological procedures in some of the forms of the verb with 2nd radical *w* or *y*:

Before embarking upon establishing the rules of the phonological changes due to the glide, it can be remarked that most of the procedures concerning the sequences of the verb with 2nd radical *w* concern as well the sequences of the verb with 2nd radical *y*. It shall be observed in this analysis that three usual changes can be applied concerning the verb with 2nd radical *w* or *y*. In some of its forms, it can have its glide changed into another segment, have it elided or retained. Another change that can affect the glide is as well the transfer of its vowel to the segment preceding it, but this occurs only on the condition that this segment is vowelless or that it has a vowel that is deemed heavy on it. The following forms, sequences and rules are presented:

5.5.1. The 3rd persons of the perfect of the verb with 2nd radical *w* or *y:* the sequence of the vowelled 2nd weak radical preceded by a fatḥa: the change of the vowelled weak radical into an *ā*.

5.5.2. The persons in the perfect of the verb with 2nd radical *w* or *y* in which the vowelled pronoun of the agent is suffixed: the sequence of the vowelless 2nd radical *ā* (that is substituted for the 2nd weak radical) preceded by a fatḥa and followed by the vowelless 3rd radical: the elision of the *ā* and the change of the 1st radical's fatḥa into another vowel.

5.5.3. The imperfect of the verb with 2nd radical *w* or *y* of the conjugation *yafᶜalu:* the sequence of the 2nd weak radical vowelled by a fatḥa and preceded by a sukūn: the transfer of the fatḥa to the vowelless segment preceding it and the change of the vowelled weak radical into an *ā* in all forms with the remark that the *ā* is elided in the imperfect forms of the fem. pl. in which the vowelled *–n, the -na*, is suffixed to.

5.5.4. The imperfect of the verb with 2nd radical *w* of the conjugation *yaf^{c}ulu:* the sequence of the 2nd radical *w* vowelled by a ḍamma and preceded by a sukūn: the transfer of the ḍamma to the vowelless segment preceding it, the change of the *wu* into an *ū* with the remark that the *-ū* is elided in the forms of the fem. pl. in which the vowelled *–n, the -na*, is suffixed to.

5.5.5. The imperfect of the verb with 2nd radical *y* of the conjugation *yaf^{c}ilu:* the sequence of the 2nd radical *y* vowelled by a kasra and preceded by a sukūn: the transfer of the kasra to the vowelless segment preceding it and the change of the *yi* into an *ī* in all forms with the remark that the *ī* is elided in the imperfect forms of the fem. pl. in which the vowelled *–n, the -na*, is suffixed to.

5.5.6. The passive participle of the verb with 2nd radical *w* *maf^c(u)wlun/ maf^c(u)ūlun:* the sequence of the 2nd radical *w* vowelled by a ḍamma, preceded by a sukūn and followed by the infixed vowelless *ū:* the transfer of the ḍamma to the vowelless segment preceding it, the change of the *wu* into an *ū* and the elision of one of the wāws.

5.5.7. The passive participle of the verb with 2nd radical *y* *maf^c(u)wlun/ maf^c(u)ūlun:* the sequence of the 2nd radical *y* vowelled by a ḍamma, preceded by a sukūn and followed by the infixed vowelless *ū:* the transfer of the ḍamma to the vowelless segment preceding it, the change of the ḍamma into a kasra, the elision of the infixed *ū* or the 2nd radical *y,* and the change of the *y* into an *ī* or the *ū* into an *ī* respectively.

5.5.8. The imperative of the verb with 2nd radical *w* or *y:* the sequence of the 2nd vowelled radical *w* or *y* that is preceded by a sukūn: the transfer of the vowel to the vowelless segment preceding it, the lengthening of the vowel into an *ū* or an *ī* respectively, and the elision of the *ū* or *ī* in both the 3rd person of the masc. sing. and the 3rd person of the fem. pl. and its retaining in the remaining persons.

5.5.9. The active participle of the verb with 2nd radical *w* or *y:* the sequence of the 2nd radical *w* or *y* vowelled by a kasra and preceded by a vowelless *ā:* the change of the *wi* or *yi* into *ʾi* respectively.

5.5.10. Anomalous cases of active participles of the verb with 2nd radical *w:* the sequence of the 2nd radical *w* vowelled by a kasra and preceded by a vowelless *ā* in them: the elision of the *w* or the transposition of segments together with the elision of the glide.

5.5.11. The verbal noun of Form I of the verb with 2nd radical *w* or *y:* the sequence in which the 2nd radical *w* or *y* is vowelless and preceded by a fatḥa: the soundness of the *w* or *y.*

5.5.12. The verbal nouns of Form IV *ʾifᶜ(a)ālun* and Form X *ʾistifᶜ(a)ālun* of the verb with 2nd radical *w:* the sequence in which the *w* is vowelled by a fatḥa and preceded by a sukūn: the transfer of the *w's* fatḥa to the segment preceding it, the change of the *w* into an *ā,* the elision of one of the alifs and the compensation with the *tāʾ marbūṭa.*

5.5.13. The passive voice of the perfect of the verb with 2nd radical *w* or *y:* the sequence of the 2nd radical *w* or *y* vowelled by a kasra and preceded by a ḍamma: the transfer of the kasra to the 1st radical and hence the change of the 1st radical's ḍamma into a kasra, the change of the *w* into a *y* or the *y* into an *ī* respectively, or the elision of the 2nd radical *w's* or *y's* kasra and the lengthening of the ḍamma preceding it into an *ū.*

5.5.14. The passive voice of the imperfect of the verb with 2nd radical *w* or *y:* the sequence of the 2nd radical *w* or *y* vowelled by a fatḥa and preceded by a sukūn: the transfer of the fatḥa to the 1st vowelless radical and the change of the *w* or the *y* into an *ā.*

5.5.15. The noun of place of the verb with 2nd radical *w:* the sequence of the 2nd radical *w* vowelled by a fatḥa and preceded by a sukūn: the transfer of the fatḥa to the vowelless segment preceding it and the change of the *wa* into an *ā*

5.5.1. The 3rd persons of the perfect with 2nd radical w or y: the sequence of the vowelled 2nd weak radical preceded by a fatḥa: the change of the vowelled weak radical into an ā:

The verb with 2nd radical *w* is first discussed and then the verb with 2nd radical *y*.

5.5.1.1. The verb with 2nd radical w:

The verb with 2nd radical *w* is divided in the perfect between the conjugation *faᶜala* in which the 2nd radical is vowelled by a fatḥa and the conjugation *faᶜula* in which it is vowelled by a ḍamma. In both these cases the vowelled *w* is changed into an *ā*.

1- The conjugation faᶜala:

In the conjugation *faᶜal*a, the 2nd radical *w* is vowelled by a fatḥa and preceded by one, which results in the change of the *wa* into an *ā* (cf. Ibn Ǧinnī, *Munṣif I,* 247, Åkesson, *Ibn Masᶜūd* 282-284: fol. 27a-27b).

The procedure is then the following:

-awa → *- (a)ā*

It is remarked that *qawala* with the 2nd radical *w* vowelled by a fatḥa and preceded by one becomes *q(a)āla* "to say" with the *wa* changed into an *ā*.

The 3rd person of the fem. sing. is *q(a)āla-t* and the 3rd person of the masc. pl. *q(a)āl(u)-ū*.

2- The conjugation *faᶜula:*

In the conjugation *faᶜula* the 2nd radical *w* is vowelled by a ḍamma and is preceded by a fatḥa, which results in the change of the *wu* into an *ā* (cf. Ibn Ǧinnı, *Munṣif I,* 247, Åkesson, *Ibn Masᶜūd* 282-284: fol. 27a-27b).

The procedure is then the following:

-awu → *-(a)ā*

It is noted as an example that *ṭawula* with the 2nd radical *w* vowelled by ḍamma and preceded by a fatḥa becomes *ṭ(a)āla* "to become long" with the *wu* changed into an *ā*.

The 3rd person of the fem. sing. is *ṭ(a)āla-t* and of the 3rd person of the masc. pl. *ṭ(a)āl(u)-ū*.

3- The conjugation *faᶜila:*

In the conjugation *faᶜila* the 2nd radical *w* is vowelled by a kasra and is preceded by fatḥa, which results in the change of the *wi* into an *ā* (cf. Ibn Ǧinnī, *Munṣif I,* 247).

The procedure is then the following:

-awi → *-(a)ā*

It is observed as an example that *ḫawifa* with the 2nd radical *w* vowelled by kasra and preceded by a fatḥa becomes *ḫ(a)āfa* "to be afraid" with the *wi* changed into an *ā*.

The 3rd person of the fem. sing. is *ḫ(a)āfa-t* and of the 3rd person of the masc. pl. *ḫ(a)āf(u)-ū*.

5.5.1.2. The verb with 2nd radical y:

The verb with 2nd radical *y* is divided in the perfect between the conjugation *fa*ᶜ*ala* in which the 2nd radical is vowelled by a fatḥa and the conjugation *fa*ᶜ*ila* in which it is vowelled by a kasra. In both these cases the vowelled *y* is changed into an *ā*.

*1- The conjugation fa*ᶜ*ala:*

The same phonological change that is carried out in the verb with 2nd radical *w* of the conjugation *fa*ᶜ*ala* (cf. par. 5.5.1.1.: 1) is carried out in the verb with 2nd radical *y* of the same conjugation. In this case, the *y*, which is vowelled by a fatḥa and preceded by one, is changed into an *ā* (cf. Ibn Ǧinnı, *Munṣif I*, 247, Åkesson, *Ibn Mas*ᶜ*ūd* 282-284: fol. 27a-27b).

The procedure is then the following:

-aya → *-(a)ā*

An example is *bayaᶜa* with the 2nd radical *y* vowelled by a fatḥa and preceded by one, which becomes *b(a)āᶜa* "to buy" with the *ya* changed into an *ā*.

The 3rd person of the fem. sing. is *b(a)āᶜa-t* and of the 3rd person of the masc. pl. *b(a)āᶜ(u)-ū*.

2- The conjugation faᶜila:

In the conjugation *faᶜila* the 2nd radical *y* is vowelled by a kasra and preceded by a fatḥa, which results in the change of the *yi* into an *ā*.

The procedure is then the following:

-ayi → *-(a)ā*

An example is *hayiba* with the 2nd radical *y* vowelled by a kasra and preceded by a fatḥa, which becomes *h(a)āba* "to be afraid" with the *yi* changed into an *ā*.

The 3rd person of the fem. sing. is *h(a)āba-t* and of the 3rd person of the masc. pl. *h(a)āb(u)-ū*.

5.5.2. The persons in the perfect of the verb with 2nd radical w or y in which the vowelled pronoun of the agent is suffixed: the sequence of the vowelless 2nd radical ā (that is substituted for the 2nd weak radical) preceded by a fatḥa and followed by the vowelless 3rd radical: the elision of the ā and the change of the 1st radical's fatḥa into another vowel:

In the 1st persons of the sing. and pl. and the 2nd persons of the masc. and fem. sing. and pl. of perfect verbs with 2nd radical *w* or *y*, the vowelled pronoun of the agent, namely the *-tu* "1st sing.", the *-nā* "1st pl.", the *-ta* "2nd masc. sing.", the *-ti* "2nd fem. sing.", the *-tumā* "2nd /dual", the *-tum* "2nd masc. pl." and the *-tunna* "2nd fem. pl."., are suffixed to the forms. As already mentioned, the 2nd weak radical, whether it is a *w* or *y*, is changed into a vowelless *ā* on account of the influence of the fatḥa preceding it and of its vowelling (cf. par. 5.5.1.). The vowelless *ā* becomes in these mentioned persons connected to the vowelless 3rd radical. This combination of two vowelless segments gives rise to the following procedures: the first is the elision of the 2nd changed radical *ā* and the second is the change of the 1st radical's vowel, namely the fatḥa, into another vowel that can in some cases give notice in its nature of the elided 2nd weak radical, whether it is a *w* or *y*, or of the underlying vowel of the 2nd radical that marks the conjugation. The cases are discussed in the following paragraphs.

5.5.2.1. The verb with 2nd radical w:

The conjugations that are taken up are *fa^cala* and *fa^cila.*

1- The conjugation fa^cala:

An example is *qawala* "he said" that belongs to the conjugation *fa^cala yaf^culu* and not to the conjugation *fa^cula yaf^culu* (cf. Ibn Ǧinnī, *Munṣif I,* 236-237, Bakkūš, *Taṣrīf* 142-143, Bohas/Kouloughli, *Linguistic* 79) to which one of the pronouns of the agent, e.g. the *-na* of the 3rd person of the fem. pl. is suffixed to. The procedure is the following (cf. Åkesson, *Ibn Mas^cūd* 288: fol. 29b, Bakkūš, *Taṣrīf* 136): *qawal-na* with the 2nd radical *w* vowelled by a fatḥa and preceded by one becomes *q(a)āl-na* with the *wa* changed into an *ā.* As there is in *q(a)āl-na* a cluster of two vowelless segments, the *ā* and the *l,* the *ā* is elided so that it becomes *qal-na.* It can be observed that what seems peculiar is that the fatḥa of the 1st radical *q* in *qal-na* is replaced by a ḍamma to give notice of the elided 2nd radical *w,* namely *qul-na.*

The same procedure is carried out when the remaining pronouns of the agent are suffixed, namely *qawal-tu* "I said" resulting in *qul-tu, qawal-nā* "we said" resulting in *qul-nā, qawal-ta* "you said /masc. sing." resulting in *qul-ta, qawal-ti* "you said /fem. sing." resulting in *qul-ti, qawal-tumā* "you said /dual" resulting in *qul-tumā, qawal-tum* "you said /masc. pl."

resulting in *qul-tum* and *qawal-tunna* "you said /fem. pl." resulting in *qul-tunna.*

<u>*2- The conjugation faᶜila:*</u>

An example is *ḫawifa* "he was afraid". In the case of the suffixation of the agent pronoun to it, e.g. the *-na* of the 3rd person of the fem. pl., namely *ḫawif-na,* the following procedure is carried out (cf. Åkesson, *Ibn Masᶜūd* 288: fol. 29b): *ḫawif-na* with the 2nd radical *w* vowelled by a kasra and preceded by a fatḥa becomes *ḫ(a)āf-na* after that its *wi* is changed into an *ā.* As there is in *ḫ(a)āf-na* a cluster of two vowelless segments: the *ā* and the *f,* the *ā* is elided so that it becomes *ḫaf-na.* Then what is special for it is that the fatḥa of the 1st radical is replaced by a kasra, which is underlyingly the vowel of the 2nd radical *w* marking the conjugation *faᶜila,* so that it becomes *ḫif-na.*

<u>*5.5.2.2. The verb with 2nd radical y:*</u>

The conjugation that is discussed is *faᶜala,* e.g. *bayaᶜa* "he sold". In the case of the suffixation of the agent pronoun, e.g. the *-na* of the 3rd person of the fem. pl., the following procedure is carried out: *bayaᶜ-na* with the 2nd radical *y* vowelled by a fatḥa and preceded by one becomes *b(a)āᶜ-na* after that its *ya* is changed into an *ā.* As there is in *b(a)āᶜ-na* a cluster of two vowelless segments: the *ā* and the ᶜ, the *ā* is elided so that it becomes *baᶜ-na.* The fatḥa of the 1st radical is then replaced by a kasra to give notice that the verb is with 2nd radical *y*, so it becomes *bi*^{c}*-na.*

The same concerns the remaining pronouns with the agent suffixes, namely *baya*^{c}*-tu* "I bought" resulting in *bi*^{c}*-tu, baya*^{c}*-nā* "we bought" resulting in *bi*^{c}*-nā, baya*^{c}*-ta* "you bought /masc. sing." resulting in *bi*^{c}*-ta, baya*^{c}*-ti* "you bought /fem. sing." resulting in *bi*^{c}*-ti, baya*^{c}*-tumā* "you bought /dual" resulting in *bi*^{c}*-tumā, baya*^{c}*-tum* "you bought /masc. pl." resulting in *bi*^{c}*-tum* and *baya*^{c}*-tunna* "you bought /fem. pl." resulting in *bi*^{c}*-tunna.*

Another example with the suffixation of the agent pronoun in the 2nd person of the masc. sing., the *-ta, is sayar-ta > s(a)ār-ta > sar-ta > sir-ta* "you moved on" (cf. Bakkūš, *Taṣrīf* 139).

5.5.3. The imperfect of the verb with 2nd radical w or y of the conjugation yaf^{c}***alu: the sequence of the 2nd weak radical vowelled by a fatḥa and preceded by a sukūn: the transfer of the fatḥa to the vowelless segment preceding it and the change of the vowelled weak radical into an ā in all forms with the remark that the ā is elided in the imperfect forms of the fem. pl. in which the vowelled –n, the -na, is suffixed to:***

The verb with 2nd radical *w* is first discussed and then the verb with 2nd radical *y*.

5.5.3.1. The verb with 2nd radical w:

An example of a verb that is formed according to this conjugation is *yaḫwafu* "he is afraid". The phonological change involves two steps: the first is the transfer of the *w's* fatḥa to the vowelless 1st radical *ḫ* preceding it, which results in *yaḫawfu,* and the second one is the change of the vowelless *w* into an *ā* on account of the influence of the fatḥa preceding it, which results in *yaḫ(a)āfu.* These two steps answer to two different principles: the first is that when the glide is vowelled and follows a sukūn its vowel is shifted to the vowelless segment preceding it and the second is that when the glide is vowelless and is preceded by a fatḥa it can be changed into an *ā*.

It can be remarked concerning the 2nd person and 3rd person of the fem. pl. to which the vowelled *–n, the –na,* is suffixed to, namely *taḫ(a)āf-na* "you are afraid /fem. pl." and *yaḫ(a)āf-na* "they are afraid /fem. pl.", that the 3rd radical becomes vowelless through the suffixation. This entails a cluster of two vowelless segments, the *ā* and the *f,* which is the reason why the *ā* is elided resulting in *taḫaf-na* and *yaḫ(a)f-na.*

5.5.3.2. The verb with 2nd radical y:

An example of a verb that is formed according to this conjugation is *yahyabu* "he is afraid". A study of the phonological changes shows the following: *yahyabu* with the

2nd radical *y* vowelled by a fatḥa preceded by a sukūn becomes *yahaybu* after that the *y's* fatḥa is shifted to the 1st radical. In *yahaybu* we have the vowelless *y* preceded by a fatḥa which forces the change of the *y* into an *ā* so that it becomes *yaḫ(a)ābu.*

Alike the verb with 2nd radical *w* of the same conjugation (cf. par. 5.5.3.: 1.), the *ā* is elided in the 2nd and 3rd person of the fem. pl. of the verb of this conjugation for the same reason. Hence *tahab-na* "you are afraid /fem. pl." is said instead of *tah(a)āb-na* and *yahab-na* "they are afraid /fem. pl." instead of *yah(u)āb-na.*

5.5.4. The imperfect of the verb with 2nd radical w of the conjugation yafᶜulu: the sequence of the 2nd radical w vowelled by a ḍamma and preceded by a sukūn: the transfer of the ḍamma to the vowelless segment preceding it, the change of the wu into an ū with the remark that the -ū is elided in the forms of the fem. pl. in which the vowelled –n, the -na, is suffixed to:

In the imperfect that is formed according to *yafᶜulu,* the 2nd radical *w* is vowelled by a ḍamma and preceded by a sukūn, e.g. *yaqwulu* "he says". The phonological procedure that is carried out implies the transfer of the ḍamma of the 2nd radical *w* to the 1st vowelless radical, and the change of the *w* into an *ū* on account of the influence of the ḍamma (cf. Ibn Ǧinnī, *Munṣif I,*

247). An example is *yaqwulu* that has the 2nd radical *w* vowelled by a ḍamma and preceded by a sukūn. It becomes *yaquwlu* after that the *w's* ḍamma is shifted to the vowelless *q*. As the vowelless *w* is preceded by a ḍamma in it, the *w* is changed into an *ū* so that it becomes *yaq(u)ūlu.*

It is observed that as with *taḫ(a)āf-na* which results in *taḫaf-na* "you are afraid /fem. pl." and *yaḫ(a)āf-na* which results in *yaḫaf-na* "they are afraid /fem. pl." with the elision of the *ā* (cf. par. 5.5.3.: 1), the *ū* is elided in the 2nd and 3rd person of the fem. pl. of the verb of this conjugation for the same reason. Hence *taqul-na* "you say /fem. pl." is said instead of *taq(u)ūl-na* and *yaqul-na* "they say /fem. pl." instead of *yaq(u)ūl-na.* The procedure that is carried out form the underlying form *yaqwul-na* to the result *yaqul-na* is the following (cf. Åkesson, *Ibn Mas*ᶜ*ūd* 290: fol. 30a): *yaqwul-na* with the 2nd radical *w* vowelled by a ḍamma and preceded by a sukūn becomes *yaquwl-na* after that the *w's* ḍamma is shifted to the vowelless *q*. As there is in it a cluster of two vowelless segments, the *w* and the *l,* the *w* is elided so that it becomes *yaqul-na.*

According to a modern theory, the *w* in *yaquwl-na* is said to be shortened into a ḍamma, which is the case when the *w* is followed by a sukūn (cf. Bakkūš, *Taṣrīf* 136).

5.5.5. The imperfect of the verb with 2nd radical y of the conjugation yafᶜilu: the sequence of the 2nd radical y vowelled by a kasra and preceded by a sukūn: the transfer of the kasra to the vowelless segment preceding it and the change of the yi into an ī in all forms with the remark that the ī is elided in the imperfect forms of the fem. pl. in which the vowelled –n, the -na, is suffixed to:

In the conjugation *yafᶜilu,* the 2nd radical *y* is vowelled by a kasra and is preceded by a sukūn. An example is *yabyiᶜu* "he sells" (cf. Åkesson, *Ibn Masᶜūd* 286: fol. 29a, Bakkūš, *Taṣrīf* 62). The phonological change that is carried out in it implies the transfer of the kasra of the 2nd radical *y* to the 1st vowelless radical resulting in the lengthening of the *y*. This phonological procedure answers to a principle that when the glide is vowelled and follows a sukūn, its vowel is shifted to the vowelless segment preceding it.

Thus:

- *ᵒyi* → *-iy*

(ᵒ stands for vowelless segment)

This can be illustrated as follows: *yabyiᶜu* with the 2nd radical *y* vowelled by a kasra and preceded by a sukūn becomes *yabiyᶜu* after that the *y's* kasra is shifted to the *b.* As the vowelless *y* is preceded by a kasra in it, the *y* is changed into an *ī* so that it becomes *yab(i)ī^{c}u.*

The *ī* is elided in the 2nd and 3rd person of the fem. pl. of the verb of this conjugation. Hence *tabi^c-na* "you sell /fem. pl." is said instead of *tab(i)ī^c-na* and *yabi^c-na* "they sell /fem. pl." instead of *yab(i)ī^c-na.* Hence *yabyi^c-na* with the 2nd radical *y* vowelled by a kasra and preceded by a sukūn becomes *yabiy^c-na* after that the *y's* kasra is shifted to the *b.* As there is in it a cluster of two vowelless segments, the *y* and ^{c}, the *y* is elided so that it becomes *yabi^c-na.*

5.5.6. *The passive participle of the verb with 2nd radical w maf^c(u)wlun / maf^c(u)ūlun: the sequence of the 2nd radical w vowelled by a ḍamma, preceded by a sukūn and followed by the infixed vowelless ū: the transfer of the ḍamma to the vowelless segment preceding it, the change of the wu into an ū and the elision of one of the wāws:*

In the pattern of the passive participle form *maf^{c}uwlun / maf^c(u)ūlun,* e.g. *maqwuwlun / maqw(u)ūlun* "what is said", the first step of the phonological change is that the ḍamma of the 2nd radical *w* is shifted to the vowelless segment preceding it (cf. Åkesson, *Ibn Mas^{c}ūd* 292: fol. 31a).

The phonological change can be illustrated as follows:

- ^{o}*wu* → *-uw*

(^{o} stands for vowelless segment)

Thus *maqw(u)ūlun* with the 2nd radical *w* vowelled by a ḍamma and preceded by a sukūn becomes *maquwūlun* after that the *w's* ḍamma is shifted to the *q*.

At this point in the treatment, two different analyses can be mentioned which lead *maquwūlun* to the result *maq(u)ūlun.* The steps that are involved in them refer to Sībawaihi's and al-Aḫfaše's different theories (for discussions see Zamaḫšarī, 180-181, Ibn Yaᶜīš, X, 78-81, Åkesson, *Ibn Masᶜūd* 292: fol. 31a, Howell, IV, fasc. I, 1498-1501).

According to the theory of Sībawaihi, *maquwūlun* which presents a cluster of two vowelless wāws, the *w* preceded by a ḍamma and the *ū,* becomes *maquwlun* after that the infixed wāw, i.e. the *ū,* is elided. According to him, *maquwlun* is formed according to the pattern *mafuᶜlun.* As the vowelless *w* is preceded by a ḍamma, the *w* is changed into an *ū* so that it becomes *maq(u)ūlun.*

According to Sībawaihi it is the infixed wāw: the *ū,* that is elided from *maquwūlun* on account of the principle that the elision of the added segment, - by which he means the infix in this form -, is more prior than the elision of a radical.

Al-Aḫfaš's approach is different as he considers that in *maquwūlun* it is the 2nd radical *w* that is elided and not the infixed wāw as Sībawaihi believes it to be. So according to him *maquwlun* > *maq(u)ūlun* is formed according to the pattern *maf(u)ūlun,* and not *mafuᶜlun* as according to Sībawaihi's theory. Al-Aḫfaš considers that it is 2nd radical *w* that is elided because he adheres to the principle that the added segment, the *ū,* is an infix marking the passive participle and the marker is not to be elided. Sībawaihi's answer to this argument is that the marker is not to be elided if it is the only marker in the form, but it can be elided if there is another marker in the word, which is the case here, as we have the *m* prefix.

5.5.7. The passive participle of the verb with 2nd radical y mafᶜ(u)wlun / mafᶜ(u)ūlun: the sequence of the 2nd radical y vowelled by a ḍamma, preceded by a sukūn and followed by the infixed vowelless ū: the transfer of the ḍamma to the vowelless segment preceding it, the change of the ḍamma into a kasra, the elision of the infixed ū or the 2nd radical y, and the change of the y into an ī or the ū into an ī respectively:

An example of a passive participle of a verb with 2nd radical *y* is *maby(u)ūᶜun* "sold". The 1st step of the phonological procedure that is carried out in it is the following (cf. Åkesson, *Ibn Masᶜūd* 292: fol. 31a): *maby(u)wᶜun* > *maby(u)ūᶜun* with the 2nd radical *y* vowelled by a ḍamma and preceded by a sukūn becomes *mabuyw^cun* and then *mabuyū^cun* after that the *y's* ḍamma is shifted to the *b*.

As with the passive participle with 2nd radical *w* *maqw(u)ūlun* (cf. par. 5.5.6.), both Sībawaihi's and al-Aḫfaše's differences of opinions concerning the phonological changes that are carried out from *mabuyū^cun* to the result *mab(i)ī^cun,* are applied (for discussions see Zamaḫšarī, 180-181, Ibn Ya^cīš, X, 78-81, Åkesson, *Ibn Mas^cūd* 292: fols. 31a-31b, Howell, IV, fasc. I, 1498-1501).

They can be illustrated as the following:

According to Sībawaihi, *mabuyū^cun* that has a cluster of a vowelless *y* and *ū* becomes *mabuy^cun* after the elision of the infixed *ū*. As there is in it a vowelless *y* preceded by a ḍamma, the ḍamma is changed into a kasra so that it becomes *mabiy^cun.* So according to his theory, *mabiy^cun* is formed according to *mafi^clun.* It can be observed that in *mabiy^cun,* the vowelless *y* is preceded by a kasra, which is the reason why the *y* is changed into an *ī*, namely *mab(i)ī^cun.*

According to al-Aḫfaš, *mabuyū^cun* which has a cluster of a vowelless *y* and *ū* becomes *mabu(ū)^cun* after that its 2nd radical *y* is elided. Then the ḍamma of the *b* is replaced by a kasra as an indication of the elided *y* so that it becomes *mabiū^cun.* As there is in it a disliked combination of an *ū* preceded by a kasra, the *ū* is changed into an *ī* so that it becomes *mab(i)īᶜun*. So according to his theory, *mab(i)īᶜun* is formed according to *maf(i)īlun*.

An analysis of both these theories shows that according to Sībawaihi's, it is the infixed *ū* that is elided from *mabuyūᶜun* before that the other changes are carried out in it whereas according to al-Aḫfaš it is the 2nd radical *y* that is elided. As for the reasons why the infixed segment is elided in the first case and the radical in the other, they are the same as those concerning *maqwuwlun / maqw(u)ūlun* (cf. 5.5.6.).

5.5.8. The imperative of the verb with 2nd radical w or y: the sequence of the 2nd vowelled radical w or y that is preceded by a sukūn: the transfer of the vowel to the vowelless segment preceding it, the lengthening of the vowel into an ū or an ī respectively, and the elision of the ū or ī in both the 3rd person of the masc. sing. and the 3rd person of the fem. pl. and its retaining in the remaining persons:

The verb with 2nd radical *w* is first discussed and then the verb with 2nd radical *y*.

5.5.8.1. The verb with 2nd radical w:

In the case of the 3rd person of the masc. sing. of the imperative that is formed according to *ᵓufwul (ufᶜul)*, the 2nd radical *w* is vowelled by a ḍamma and preceded by a sukūn. The phonological changes that are carried out imply the transfer of the 2nd radical *w's* vowel to the vowelless 1st radical preceding it, the elision of the connective hamza of the imperative on account that the 1st radical is now vowelled and hence the hamza that is prefixed to hinder the word from beginning with a vowelless segment is not more needed, the change of the *w* into an *ū* and the elision of the *ū* to avoid the cluster of two vowelless segments.

An example is *ˀuqwul* that becomes *qul* "say!" (cf. Åkesson, *Ibn Masᶜūd* 290: fol. 30a, ᶜAbd al-Raḥīm, *Ṣarf* 31). The procedure is the following: *ˀuqwul* with the 2nd radical *w* vowelled by a ḍamma and preceded by a sukūn becomes *ˀuquwl* after that the *w's* ḍamma is shifted to the vowelless *q*. As the 1st radical *q* is vowelled, the connective hamza of the imperative is elided because it is not more needed, so it became *quwl*. The vowelless *w* is here preceded by a ḍamma which is why it is changed into an *ū* so it becomes *q(u)ūl*. As there is now a cluster of two vowelless segments, the *ū* and *l*, the *ū* is elided so it becomes *qul*.

The *ū* is as well elided in the 3rd person of the fem. pl. *qul-na* "Say /fem. pl." which is not said *q(u)ūl-na* to avoid the combination of the vowelless *ū* and the 3rd vowelless radical *l*.

However in the forms of the imperative to which the vowelless agent pronoun is suffixed to, namely the 2nd person of the fem. sing. with the *-ī* suffix, e.g. *q(u)ūl(i)-ī*, the dual with the *ā* suffix, e.g. *q(u)ūl(a)-ā* and the 2nd person of the masc. pl., with the *-ū* suffix, e.g. *q(u)ūl(u)-ū,* the 2nd radical *ū* is maintained. The reason is that the 3rd radical of the verb, the *l,* is not more vowelless due to the suffixation of the pronoun, but vowelled with a vowel that agrees with the nature of the suffix, and hence the situation of having two vowelless segments which would force the elision is not actual in this case.

5.5.8.2. The verb with 2nd radical y:

The phonological changes are the same as those concerning the 3rd person of the masc. sing. of the imperative of verbs with 2nd radical *w* that are formed according to *ʾufᶜul* (cf. above), except that conjugation is instead *ʾifᶜil,* e.g. *ʾibyiᶜ* "sell!". Hence the kasra of the *y* is shifted to the vowelless segment preceding it, namely *ʾibiyᶜ*, the connective hamza is elided, namely *biyᶜ*, the *y* is changed into an *ī,* namely *b(i)īᶜ*, and is then elided, namely *biᶜ*.

The *ī* is as well elided in the 3rd person of the fem. pl. *biᶜ-na* "sell /fem. pl." which is not said *b(i)īᶜ-na* to avoid the combination of the vowelless ī and the 3rd vowelless radical ᶜ.

In the forms of the imperative to which the vowelless agent pronoun is suffixed to, namely the 2nd person of the fem. sing. with the *-ī* suffix, e.g. *b(i)yᶜ(i)-ī* > *b(i)īᶜ(i)-ī,* the dual with the ā suffix, e.g. *b(i)yᶜ(a)-ā* > *b(i)īᶜ(a)-ā* and the 2nd person of the masc. pl., with the *-ū* suffix, e.g. *b(i)y^{c}(u)-ū* > *b(i)ī^{c}(u)-ū,* the 2nd radical *y* is maintained.

5.5.9. The active participle of the verb with 2nd radical w or y: the sequence of the 2nd radical w or y vowelled by a kasra and preceded by a vowelless ā: the change of the wi or yi into ᵓi respectively:

The verb with 2nd radical *w* is first discussed and then the verb with 2nd radical *y*.

5.5.9.1. The verb with 2nd radical w:

The active participle's form of the verb with 2nd radical *w* is *f(a)ā^{c}ilun*. In this form the 2nd radical *w* is vowelled by a kasra and preceded by a vowelless *ā*. The phonological procedure that is carried out in it implies that the *wi* is changed into *ᵓi* (cf. ^{c}Abd al-Raḥīm, *Ṣarf* 80). An example is *q(a)āwilun* that becomes *q(a)āᵓilun* "a sayer".

The phonological procedure is different according to Ibn Mas^{c}ūd (cf. Åkesson, *Ibn Mas^{c}ūd* 290: fol. 30b). He adheres to the theory that *q(a)āwilun* with the 2nd radical *w* vowelled by a kasra is influenced by the fatḥa preceding the *ā,* and the *ā* is not taken into account because of its vowellessness. So the *wi* is changed into an *ā* on account of the influence of the fatḥa preceding it, so that it becomes *q(a)āālun.* The reason why one of the alifs is not dropped resulting in *q(a)ālun,* is to prevent that the active participle is mixed up with the perfect *q(a)āla* "he said". The 2nd *ā* is therefore changed into a hamza to prevent the combination of two vowelless alifs, so it became *q(a)āᵓilun.*

5.5.9.2. *The verb with 2nd radical y:*

Alike the active participle of the verb with 2nd radical *w* that is formed according to *fāᶜilun* (cf. par. 5.5.9.: 1), the active participle of the verb with 2nd radical *y,* has its *yi* changed into *ᵓi* instead. An example is *b(a)āyiᶜun* with the 2nd radical *y* vowelled by a kasra and preceded by an *ā* that becomes *b(a)āᵓiᶜun* "a seller" after that the *yi* is changed into an *ᵓi.*

5.5.10. *Anomalous cases of active participles of the verb with 2nd radical w: the sequence of the 2nd radical w vowelled by a kasra and preceded by a vowelless ā in them: the elision of the w or the transposition of segments together with the elision of the glide:*

The cases that are discussed are those that imply the elision of the 2nd radical *w* and the transposition of the segments together with the elision.

1- The elision of the 2nd radical w:

In some cases of active participles, the 2nd weak radical is elided (cf. Åkesson, *Ibn Masᶜūd* 290-292: fol. 30b). Some examples are *h(a)āᶜun* "vomitting" used instead of *h(a)āʾiᶜun* underlyingly *h(a)āwiᶜun* from *hawaᶜa* "to vomit", *l(a)āᶜun* "suffering" used instead of *l(a)āʾiᶜun* underlyingly *l(a)āwiᶜun* from *lawaᶜa* "to suffer, burn" and *h(a)ārun* "undermined" used instead of *h(a)āʾirun* underlyingly *h(a)āwirun* from *hawara* "to demolish". The variant *h(a)ārun* (instead of *h(a)āʾirun)* with the elision of the *ʾi* occurs in the genetive in the sur. 9: 109 *(ᶜalā šafā ǧurufin hārin)* "On an undermined sand-cliff". Hence these examples of active participles are formed according to the pattern *fālun* and not *fāᶜilun.* The phonological changes concerning one of these examples, e.g. *h(a)āwiᶜun* that becomes *h(a)āᶜun* "vomitting", are the following: *h(a)āwiᶜun* with the 2nd radical *w* vowelled by a kasra and preceded by an *ā* becomes *h(a)āʾiᶜun* after that the *wi* is changed into an *ʾi.* The procedure resulting in the elision of the 2nd weak radical is that the 2nd radical *w* vowelled by a kasra in *h(a)āwiᶜun* is influenced by the fatḥa of the *h* preceding the *ā,* on account of the principle that the *ā* is not taken into account because of its vowellessness. So the *wi* is changed into an *ā* so that it becomes *h(a)āāᶜun.* As there is in it a cluster of two vowelless alifs, one of them is elided so that it becomes *h(a)āᶜun.*

2- The transposition of segments together with the elision of the glide:

The transposition of the segments is carried out in some examples (for an example concerning the active participle of a verb with 1st radical *w,* e.g. *w(a)āḥidun* > *ḥ(a)ādin* see par. 5.2.1.6.).

An example is *š(a)āwikun* "sharp" in which the 2nd radical *w* changes place with the 3rd radical (cf. Ibn Manẓūr, IV, 2362-2363). It becomes at first *š(a)ākiwun* formed according to the pattern *f(a)āliᶜun* instead of *f(a)āᶜilun.* As the form ends with a weak radical, it resembles the active participle of verbs with 3rd weak radical, e.g. the underlying forms *r(a)āmiyun* for the nominative and *r(a)āmiyin* for the genitive which becomes *r(a)āmin* "one who is throwing" for both the nominative and the genitive (cf. Wright, II, 90). This is how it is understood that the variant *š(a)ākiwun* has its last radical elided and the *tanwin* "nunation" is given to its 2nd radical on the analogy of this category of forms, so that it becomes *š(a)ākin.* It occurs in this verse recited by Ṭarīf b. Tamīm al-ᶜAmbarī al-Tamīmi, cited by Sībawaihi, II, 419, Ibn Ǧinnī, *Munṣif II,* 53, III, 66, Howell, IV, fasc. I, 1494, Åkesson, *Ibn Masᶜūd* 317: (292):

> *"Fa-taᶜarrafūnī ᵓinnanī ᵓanā ḏākumu*
> *sākin silāḥī fī l-ḥawādiṯi muᶜlimu".*
> Then seek to know me: verily that I, this one, [am such that]
> sharp is my weapon in mishaps, am a bearer of the cognizance, or badge, or device, of the valiant".

5.5.11. The verbal noun of Form I of the verb with 2nd radical w or y: the sequence in which the 2nd radical w or y is vowelless and preceded by a fatḥa: the soundness of the w or y:

The verbal noun of Form I of the verb with 2nd radical *w* or *y* is *faᶜlun.* In both these forms the 2nd weak radical is vowelless and preceded by a fatḥa, which is the reason why it remains sound. An example of a verbal noun with 2nd radical *w* is *qawlun* "a saying" and with 2nd radical *y bayᶜun* "a selling".

5.5.12. The verbal nouns of Form IV ᵓifᶜ(a)ālun and Form X ᵓistifᶜ(a)ālun of the verb with 2nd radical w: the sequence in which the w is vowelled by a fatḥa and preceded by a sukūn: the transfer of the w's fatḥa to the segment preceding it, the change of the w into an ā, the elision of one of the alifs and the compensation with the tāᵓ marbūṭa:

In some examples of verbal forms of Form IV *ᵓīfᶜ(a)ālun,* e.g. *ᵓiqw(a)āmun* "the act of being constant (in prayer)", the 2nd radical *w* is vowelled by a fatḥa and preceded by a sukūn. The phonological changes that are carried out in it resulting in *ᵓiq(a)āmatun* are the following: *ᵓiqw(a)āmun* with the 2nd radical *w* vowelled by a fatḥa and preceded by a sukūn becomes at first *ᵓiqawāmun* after that the fatḥa is shifted to the vowelless *q* and then *ʾiq(a)āāmun* after that the *w* is changed into an *ā*. As there is in it a cluster of two vowelless segments, the alifs, one of them is elided resulting in *ʾiq(a)āmun,* and the *tāʾ marbūṭa* is suffixed to compensate for this elision so that it becomes *ʾiq(a)āmatun.* It can be mentioned that the *tāʾ marbūṭa* is elided from *wa-ʾiq(a)āmatu* (cf. Sībawaihi, II, 260-261, Zamaḫšarī, 179, de Sacy, I, 294, Howell, I, fasc. III 1126, fasc. IV, 1571-1572, IV, fasc. I 1424, Wright, II, 120-121), in the sur. 21: 73 *(wa-ʾiqāmu l-ṣalāti)* "to establish regular prayers", the reason being that *l-ṣalāti,* which is the second element of the construct state, is considered as a substitute that compensates for the elided *tāʾ marbūṭa* (compare the case of *ʿida l-ʾamri* in par. 5.2.1.2.).

The same phonological changes apply for Form X of the verbal noun that is formed according to *ʾistifʿ(a)ālun,* e.g. *ʾistiqw(a)āmun* that becomes *ʾistiq(a)āmatun* "the act of walking uprightly in the paths of religion". The 2nd radical *w* in *ʾistiqw(a)āmun,* which is vowelled by a fatḥa, is changed into an *ā* after that its fatḥa is shifted to the *q,* so that it becomes *ʾistiq(a)āāmun,* then one of the alifs is elided to avoid the cluster of two vowelless alifs, and the *tāʾ marbūṭa* is suffixed to the word as a compensation for this elision.

5.5.13. The passive voice of the perfect of the verb with 2nd radical w or y: the sequence of the 2nd radical w or y vowelled by a kasra and preceded by a ḍamma: the transfer of the kasra to the 1st radical and hence the change of the 1st radical's ḍamma into a kasra, the change of the w into a y or the y into an ī respectively, or the elision of the 2nd radical w's or y's kasra and the lengthening of the ḍamma preceding it into an ū:

The verb with 2nd radical *w* is discussed at first and then the verb with 2nd radical *y*.

5.5.13.1. The verb with 2nd radical w:

An example of a verb in the passive voice *fuᶜila* is *quwila* "was said". The *w* is vowelled by a kasra in it and preceded by a ḍamma, which is deemed as a heavy combination. The usual following phonological changes that are carried out in it resulting in *q(i)īla* are the following (cf. Åkesson, *Ibn Masᶜūd* 294: fol. 31b, Bakkūš, *Taṣrīf* 146, ᶜAbd al-Raḥīm, *Ṣarf* 31-32:

quwila with the 2nd radical *w* vowelled by a kasra and preceded by a ḍamma becomes *qiwla* after that the kasra of the *w* is shifted to the 1st radical and hence replaces the ḍamma. As the vowelless *w* is preceded by a kasra in it, the *w* is changed into a *y* resulting in *qiyla.* Then the vowelless *y* preceded by a kasra is lengthened into an *ī* so that it became *q(i)īla.*

According to another dialectal variant which is deemed as feeble, the *w* of *quwila* is made vowelless for the purpose of alleviation, and the variant *quwla* resulting in *q(u)ūla* occurs (cf. Åkesson, *Ibn Masᶜūd* 294: fol. 31b). This is the dialectal variant of the Banū Asad (for discussions see Bakkūš, *Taṣrīf* 146-147). The changes can be illustrated as follows:

quwila with the 2nd radical *w* vowelled by a kasra and preceded by ḍamma becomes *quwla* after that the *w's* kasra is elided to alleviate. As the vowelless *w* is preceded by a ḍamma in it, the *w* is lengthened into an *ū,* or in other words the *w* is assimilated to the ḍamma resulting in *q(u)ūla.*

According to another dialectal variant, the *ᵓišmām,* i.e. "giving the vowel preceding the glide a flavour of the ḍamma so that it notifies of the underlying form", is carried out: *q(i)īla* is said *quila.*

Hence the following variants with the vowelled pronoun of the agent in the perfect can be mentioned (cf. Sībawaihi, II, 398, Ibn Ǧinnī, *Munṣif I,* 293-295, Åkesson, *Ibn Masᶜūd* 294: fol. 31b, Howell, IV, fasc. I, 1476-1484):

Form I *quwil-na* with the *-na*	→	1- *qil-na* "were said /fem. pl."
	→	2- *qu(u)ūl-na*
	→	3- *ᵓišmām: quil-na*

5.5.13.2. The verb with 2nd radical y:

An example of a passive voice of a verb with 2nd radical *y* is *buyiᶜa* "was sold" that is formed according to *fuᶜila.* As with *quwila* (cf. above) the three variants can be applied for it. The usual phonological changes concerning the first variant are the following:

buyiᶜa with the 2nd radical *y* vowelled by a kasra and preceded by ḍamma becomes *biyᶜa* after that the kasra of the *y* is shifted to the 1st radical and hence replaces the ḍamma. As the 2nd radical vowelless *y* is preceded by a kasra in it, the *y* is lengthened into an *ī* so that it becomes *bi(ī)ᶜa.*

The two other possibilities are *b(u)ūᶜa* and with the *ʾišmām* carried out in it *buiᶜa.*

Hence the following variants with the vowelled pronoun of the agent in the perfect can be mentioned:

Form I *buyiᶜ-na* with the *-na* → 1- *biᶜ-na* "were sold /fem. pl.".

→ 2- *b(u)ūᶜ-na*

→ 3- *ʾišmām: buiᶜ-na*

5.5.14. The passive voice of the imperfect of the verb with 2nd radical w or y: the sequence of the 2nd radical w or y vowelled by a fatḥa and preceded by a sukūn: the transfer of the fatḥa to the 1st vowelless radical and the change of the w or the y into an ā:

The imperfect of the passive voice of the verb with 2nd radical *w* or *y* is formed according to *yuf*^{c}*alu*. The sequence in this form is that of a glide vowelled by a fatḥa and preceded by a sukūn. The first rule that is taken into account is that the fatḥa of the glide is shifted to the vowelless segment preceding it. This in its turn leads to a second rule that is the change of the glide into an *ā*.

An example of a verb with 2nd radical *w* is *yuqwalu* which becomes *yuq(a)ālu* "is said". On examination, the phonological changes are the following:

yuqwalu with the 2nd radical *w* vowelled by a fatḥa preceded by a sukūn becomes *yuqawlu* after that the *w's* fatḥa is shifted to the 1st radical *q*. As *yuqawlu* has its vowelless *w* preceded by a fatḥa, it becomes *yuq(a)ālu* with the *w* changed into an *ā*. This change of the vowelless *w* into an *ā* may be said to be triggered by the fatḥa preceding the *w*.

An example of a verb with 2nd radical *y* is *yubya*^{c}*u* which becomes *yub(a)ā*^{c}*u* "is sold". On examination, *yubya*^{c}*u* with its

2nd radical *y* vowelled by a fatḥa preceded by a sukūn becomes *yubay*^{c}*u* with the *y's* fatḥa shifted to the 1st radical *b.*

And *yubay*^{c}*u* with the vowelless *y* preceded by a fatḥa becomes *yub(a)ā*^{c}*u* with the *y* changed into an *ā.*

5.5.15. The noun of place of the verb with 2nd radical w: the sequence of the 2nd radical w vowelled by a fatḥa and preceded by a sukūn: the transfer of the fatḥa to the vowelless segment preceding it and the change of the w into an ā:

The pattern of the noun of place of the verb with with 2nd radical *w* is *maf*^{c}*alun.* An example is *maqwalun* resulting in *maq(a)ālun* "speech" (cf. Åkesson, *Ibn Mas*^{c}*ūd* 292: fol. 31b). The sequence is that of a *w* vowelled by a fatḥa and preceded by a sukūn. Alike the cases analysed in par. 5.5.14., the first rule that is taken into account is the transfer of the glide's fatḥa to the vowelless segment preceding it, and the second rule is the change of the glide into an *ā.*

Thus *maqwalun* with the 2nd radical *w* vowelled by a fatḥa and preceded by a sukūn becomes at first *maqawlun* with the *w's* fatḥa shifted to the 1st radical *q.* As *maqawlun* has its vowelless *w* preceded by a fatḥa, it becomes *maq(a)ālun* with the *w* changed into an *ā.*

5.6. A few remarks concerning some homonymous forms

One form can be common for two different forms, and it is only by *al-farq al-taqdīrī* "the theoretical difference" existing between both their underlying forms that it is possible to separate the forms from each other.

An example of such a form referring to a verb with 2nd radical *w* is *qul-na* which is common for both the 3rd person of the fem. pl. of the perfect "they said, fem. pl." and the 2nd person of the fem. pl. of the imperative "say! fem. pl.". The Arab grammarians seemed satisfied with the underlying forms of both these tenses which differenciate them from one another. As a matter of fact, the form *qul-na* referring to the 3rd person of the fem. pl. of the perfect is underlyingly *qawal-na* (for the phonological change carried out in it see par. 5.5.2.: 1) and the form *qul-na* referring to the 2nd person of the fem. pl. of the imperative is underlyingly *ʾuqwul-na* (cf. par. 5.5.8.1.).

Another example of such a form referring to a verb with 2nd radical *y* is *biʿ-na* "they sold, or they were sold /fem. pl.", which is common for the active and the passive voice. The underlying form of the active voice is *bayaʿ-na* with the *b* and the *y* vowelled by a fatḥa (for the phonological change that is carried out in it see par. 5.5.2.2.) and that of the passive voice is *buyiʿ*-

na (with the *b* vowelled by a ḍamma and the *y* vowelled by a kasra (for the phonological change see 5.5.13.2.).

6. THE CLASS OF THE VERB WITH 3RD RADICAL W OR Y

The verb with 3rd radical *w* or *y* or the defective verb is generally termed as *muᶜtal al-lām or al-nāqiṣ.*

A less well-known nomination is *ḏū l-ᵓarbaᶜa* "the one with four segments" that is given to it by Ibn Masᶜūd (Åkesson, *Ibn Masᶜūd* 326: fol. 32a), because it maintains its 3rd weak radical when the vowelled suffixed agent pronoun, namely the *-tu* "/1st person of the sing.", *-ta* "2nd person of the masc. sing.", *-ti* "2nd person of the fem. sing.", *-tumā* "2nd person of the dual", *-tum* "2nd person of the masc. pl." or *-na* "3rd person of the fem pl., is attached to it, by contrast to the verb with 2nd *w* or *y* radical that loses its 2nd weak radical in these cases, e.g. *qul-tu* "I said" underlyingly *qawal-tu* that loses the *w* radical, and hence *qul-ta* "you said /masc. sing." underlyingly *qawal-ta, qul-ti* "you said /fem. sing." underlyingly *qawal-ti, qul-tumā* "you said /dual" underlyingly *qawal-tumā, qul-tum* "you said /dual." underlyingly *qawal-tum, qawal-na* "they said /fem. pl." underlyingly *qawal-na,* etc. and *bi^c-tu* "I sold" underlyingly *baya^c-tu* that loses the *y* radical, and hence *bi^c-ta* "you said /masc. sing." underlyingly *baya^c-ta, bi^c-ti* "you said /fem. sing." underlyingly *baya^c-ti, bi^c-na* "they said /fem. pl." underlyingly *baya^c-na,* etc.

a- verb with 3rd radical w

An example of a verb with 3rd radical *w* in the 1st person of the sing. is *da^{c}aw-tu* "I called", and hence *da^{c}aw-ta* "you called /masc. sing.", *da^{c}aw-ti* "you called /fem. sing." and *da^{c}aw-na* "they called /fem. pl.". Thus:

da^{c}aw-tu	=	*fa^{c}al-tu*
da+^{c}a+w+tu	=	*fa+^{c}a+l+tu*
1 + 2 + 3 + 4 segments	=	1 + 2 + 3 + 4 segments

<u>*b- verb with 3rd radical y*</u>

An example of a verb with 3rd radical *y* in the 1st person of the sing. is *ramay-tu* "I threw", and hence *ramay-ta* "you threw /masc. sing.", *ramay-ti* "you threw /fem. sing." and *ramay-na* "they called /fem. pl.". Thus:

ramay-tu	=	*fa^{c}al-tu*
ra+ma+y+tu	=	*fa+^{c}a+l+tu*
1 + 2 + 3 + 4 segments	=	1 + 2 + 3 + 4 segments

6.1. The conjugations of the verb with 3rd radical *w*

The verb with 3rd radical *w* falls into the following conjugation:

1- *fa^{c}ala yaf^{c}ulu,* e.g. *ġazawa yaġzuwu* "to attack" that becomes after the phonological change *ġazā yaġzū.*

6.2. Examples of some derivatives and paradigms of the verb with 3rd radical *w*

An example of a verb with 3rd radical *w* in the perfect is *ġazā* "to attack" (with final *alif mamdūda).* It becomes *yaġzū* in the imperfect of the indicative active. Its imperative is *ʾuġzu,* its active participle is *ġāzin,* its *maṣdar* is *ġazwun,* its perfect passive is *ġuziya,* its imperfect is *yuġzā* and its passive participle is *maġzīyun.*

Its paradigm in the perfect, active, is as follows:

	sing.	dual	pl.
1st	*ġazaw-tu*		*ġazaw-n(a)ā*
2nd masc.	*ġazaw-ta*	*ġazaw-tum(a)ā*	*ġazaw-tum*
2nd fem.	*ġazaw-ti*	*ġazaw-tum(a)ā*	*ġazaw-tunna*
3rd masc.	*ġaz(a)ā*	*ġaz(a)-ā*	*ġaza-w*
3rd fem.	*ġaza-t*	*ġaza-t(a)ā*	*ġazaw-na*

Its imperfect in the indicative, active, is the following:

	sing.	dual	pl.
1st	*ʾaġz(u)ū*		*naġz(u)ū*
2nd masc.	*taġz(u)ū*	*taġz(u)w(a)-āni*	*taġz(u)-ūna*
2nd fem.	*taġz(i)-īna*	*taġzuw(a)-āni*	*taġz(u)-ūna*
3rd masc.	*yaġz(u)ū*	*yaǧzuw(a)-āni*	*yaġz(u)-ūna*
3rd fem.	*taġz(u)ū*	*taġzuw(a)-āni*	*yaġz(u)-ūna*

Its imperfect in the indicative, subjunctive, is the following:

1st	*ʾaġz(u)wa*		*naġz(u)wa*
2nd masc.	*taġz(u)wa*	*taġz(u)w(a)-ā*	*taġz(u)-ū*
2nd fem.	*taġz(u)wa*	*taġz(u)w(a)-ā*	*taġz(u)-ūna*
3rd masc.	*yaġz(u)wa*	*yaǧzuw(a)-ā*	*yaġz(u)-ū*
3rd fem.	*taġz(u)wa*	*taġzuw(a)-ā*	*yaġz(u)-ūna*

Its imperfect in the indicative, jussive, is the following:

1st	*ʾaġzu*		*naġzu*
2nd masc.	*taġzu*	*taġzuw(a)-ā*	*taġz(u)-ū*
2nd fem.	*taġz(i)-ī*	*taġzuw(a)-ā*	*taġz(u)-ūna*
3rd masc.	*yaġzu*	*yağzuw(a)-ā*	*yaġz(u)-ū*
3rd fem.	*taġzi*	*taġzuw(a)-ā*	*yaġz(u)-ūna*

6.3. The conjugations of the verb with 3rd radical *y*

The verb with 3rd radical *y* falls into the following conjugations:

1- *faᶜala yafᶜilu,* e.g. *ramaya yarmiyu* "to throw" that becomes after the phonological change *ramā yarmī.*

2- *faᶜala yafᶜalu,* e.g. *nahaya yanhayu* "to forbid" that becomes after the phonological change *nahā yanhā.*

3- *faᶜila yafᶜalu,* e.g. *raḍiya yarḍayu* "to consent" that becomes after the phonological change *raḍā yarḍā.*

6.4. Examples of some derivatives and paradigms of the verb with 3rd radical *y*

An example of a verb with 3rd radical *y* in the perfect is *ramaya* "to throw". It becomes *yarmī* in the imperfect of the indicative active. Its imperative is *ʾirmi,* its active participle is *rāmin,* its *maṣdar* is *ramyun,* its perfect passive is *rumiya,* its imperfect is *yurmā,* its passive participle is *marmīyun* and the nouns of time and place are *marman.*

Its paradigm in the perfect, active, is as follows:

	sing.	dual	pl.
1st	*ramay-tu*		*ramay-n(a)ā*
2nd masc.	*ramay-ta*	*ramay-tum(a)ā*	*ramay-tum*
2nd fem.	*ramay-ti*	*ramay-tum(a)ā*	*ramay-tunna*
3rd masc.	*ram(a)ā*	*ram(a)-ā*	*rama-w*
3rd fem.	*rama-t*	*rama-t(a)ā*	*ramay-na*

Its imperfect in the indicative, active, is the following:

	sing.	dual	pl.
1st	*ʾarm(i)ī*		*narm(i)ī*
2nd masc.	*tarm(i)ī*	*tarmiy(a)-āni*	*tarm(u)-ūna*
2nd fem.	*tarm(i)-īna*	*tarmiy(a)-āni*	*tarm(i)-īna*
3rd masc.	*yarm(i)ī*	*yarmiy(a)-āni*	*yarm(u)-ūna*
3rd fem.	*tarm(i)ī*	*tarmiy(a)-āni*	*yarm(i)-īna*

Its imperfect in the indicative, subjunctive, is the following:

	sing.	dual	pl.
1st	*ʾarm(i)ya*		*narm(i)ya*
2nd masc.	*tarm(i)ya*	*tarmiy(a)-ā*	*tarm(u)-ū*
2nd fem.	*tarm(i)ya*	*tarmiy(a)-ā*	*tarm(i)-īna*
3rd masc.	*yarm(i)ya*	*yarmiy(a)-ā*	*yarm(u)-ū*
3rd fem.	*tarm(i)ya*	*tarmiy(a)-ā*	*yarm(i)-īna*

Its imperfect in the indicative, jussive, is the following:

	sing.	dual	pl.
1st	*ʾarmi*		*narmi*
2nd masc.	*tarmi*	*tarmiy(a)-ā*	*tarm(u)-ū*
2nd fem.	*tarm(i)-ī*	*tarmiy(a)-ā*	*tarm(i)-īna*
3rd masc.	*yarmi*	*yarmiy(a)-ā*	*yarm(u)-ū*
3rd fem.	*tarmi*	*tarmiy(a)-ā*	*yarm(i)-īna*

6.5. Remarks concerning the phonological procedures in some of the forms of the verb with 3rd radical *w* or *y*

Most of the phonological changes that are carried out in the verb with 3rd radical *w* and some of its derivatives are similar to those that are carried out in the verb with 3rd radical *y* and some of its derivatives. The *w* or the *y* can be changed in some forms into another segment, be elided or retained. Its vowel can as well be shifted to the segment preceding it after the elision of the *w* or the *y* or its vowel can be elided and the vowel preceding it can be changed into another vowel.

Thus the following forms and sequences can be presented:

6.5.1. The 3rd person of the masc. sing. of the perfect: the sequence of the vowelled *w* or *y* preceded by a fatḥa: its change into an *ā*.

6.5.2. The 3rd person of the fem. sing. and fem. dual of the perfect: the sequence in which the vowelless *ā* (that is substituted for the glide vowelled by a fatḥa) is followed by the -*t* that marks the fem.: the elision of the *ā*.

6.5.3. The persons in the perfect to which the vowelled agent pronoun is suffixed to: the sequence of the 3rd vowelless weak radical preceded by a fatḥa: the retaining of the *w* or *y*.

6.5.4. The 3rd person of the masc pl. of the perfect of the conjugation *faᶜala:* the sequence of the 3rd radical *w* or *y* vowelled by a ḍamma (on account that it is followed by the vowelless *ū* / *w* marker of the pl.), and preceded by a fatḥa: the change of the *wu* or *yu* into an *ā* and the elision of the *ā*.

6.5.5. The 3rd person of the masc pl. of the perfect of the verb with 3rd radical *y* of the conjugation *faᶜila:* the sequence of the 3rd radical *y* vowelled by a ḍamma (on account of the vowelless *ū* / *w* marker of the pl. following it), and preceded by a kasra: the transfer of the ḍamma before the *y* and hence the change of the kasra into a ḍamma, the elision of the *y* and the lengthening of the ḍamma into an *ū* according to a theory, or the elision of the *y's* ḍamma, the elision of the *y* and the change of the kasra into a ḍamma according to another theory.

6.5.6. The persons in which no suffix is attached to the imperfect: the sequence in which the glide is vowelled by the ḍamma of the indicative and preceded by a vowel: the elision of the ḍamma.

6.5.7. The duals of the imperfect: the sequence in which the glide is vowelled by a fatḥa and preceded by a vowel: the glide's retaining.

6.5.8. The 2nd person of the fem. sing. of the imperfect of a verb with 3rd radical *y:* the sequence in which the 3rd radical *y* is vowelled by a kasra and is followed by the vowelless *ī* marker of the fem. sing.: the elision of the vowel of the *y* together with the *y*.

6.5.9. The 2nd and 3rd persons of the masc. pl. of the imperfect of a verb with 3rd radical *y:* the sequence in which the 3rd radical *y* is vowelled by a ḍamma, preceded by a kasra and followed by the vowelless *ū* marker of the masc. pl.: the elision of the ḍamma of the *y* together with the *y* and the change of the kasra into a ḍamma.

6.5.10. Form IV and other derived forms of the perfect of verbs with 3rd *w* radical to which the vowelled agent pronoun is suffixed to: the sequence of the 3rd vowelless weak radical preceded by a fatḥa: the change of the *w* into a *y*.

6.5.11. Form IV and other derived forms of the imperfect of the verbs with 3rd *w* radical: the sequence of the 3rd vowelled weak radical preceded by a kasra in them: the change of the *w* into a *y*.

6.5.12. The active participle of the verb with 3rd radical *y:* the sequence of the vowelled *y* preceded by a kasra in the definite and indefinite forms: the elision of the vowel of the *y* in the definite form, and the elision of the vowel together with the 3rd radical *y* in the nominative and genitive cases with the *tanwīn* replacing the kasra of the 2nd radical in the indefinite form.

6.5.13. The passive participle of the verb with 3rd radical *y:* the sequence of the vowelless infixed *ū* preceding the *y:* the change of the vowelless infixed *ū* into a *y*, the change of the ḍamma preceding the changed *y* into a kasra and the assimilation of the *y* to the *y*.

6.5.14. The noun of place of the verb with 3rd radical *y:* the sequence of the vowelled *y* preceded by a kasra: the change of the kasra into a fatḥa and of the *y* into an *alif maqṣūra*.

6.5.15. The jussive of the verb with 3rd radical *w* or *y:* the sequence of the vowelless *w* or *y* preceded by a vowel: the elision of the *w* or *y*.

6.5.1. The 3rd person of the masc. sing. of the perfect: the sequence of the vowelled w or y preceded by a fatḥa: its change into an ā:

The verb with 2nd radical *w* shall first be discussed and then the verb with 2nd radical *y*.

6.5.1.1. The verb with 3rd radical w:

The verb with 3rd radical *w* occurs in the 3rd person of the masc. sing. of the perfect according to the conjugation *faᶜala.* In this sequence the *w* is vowelled by a fatḥa and is preceded by one, which results in its change into an *ā* namely an *alif mamdūda* (cf. Åkesson, *Ibn Masᶜūd* 326: fol. 32a).

Thus:

-awa → *- (a)ā (alif mamdūda)*

An example of a verb with a 3rd radical *w* is *ġazawa* with the 3rd radical *w* vowelled by a fatḥa and preceded by one that becomes *ġaz(a)ā* "to raid" with the *wa* changed into *ā* [sc. *alif mamdūda]*.

6.5.1.2. The verb with 3nd y radical:

The verb with 3rd radical *y* occurs according to *faᶜala* or *faᶜila*. The *ya* in both these conjugations is changed into *ā*, namely an *alif maqṣūra* (cf. Åkesson, *Ibn Masᶜūd* 326: fol. 32a).

Thus:

-aya → *- (a)ā (alif maqṣūra)*

An example of a verb with a 3rd radical *y* formed according to *faᶜala* is *ramaya* with the 3rd radical *y* vowelled by a fatḥa and preceded by a fatḥa that becomes *ram(a)ā* "to throw" with the *ya* changed into an *ā* [sc. *alif maqṣūra]*.

Thus:

-iya → *- (a)ā (alif maqṣūra)*

An example of a verb with a 3rd radical *y* formed according to *faᶜila* is *raḍiya* with the 3rd radical *y* vowelled by a fatḥa and preceded by a kasra that becomes *raḍ(a)ā* "to consent" with the *ya* changed into *ā* [sc. *alif maqṣūra]* and the kasra changed into a fatḥa.

6.5.2. The 3rd person of the fem. sing. and fem. dual of the perfect: the sequence in which the vowelless ā (that is substituted for the glide vowelled by a fatḥa) is followed by the -t that marks the fem.: the elision of the ā:

It has been asserted previously that in the case of the 3rd person of the fem. sing. of the verb with 3rd *w* or *y* radical to which the vowelless suffix *-t* that marks the fem. is suffixed to, the 3rd weak radical is at first changed into *ā* on account of the fatḥa preceding it (for this sequence see par. 6.5.1.1., 6.5.1.2.) and the *ā* is then elided to avoid the cluster of two vowelless segments: the vowelless *ā* and the vowelless fem. marker *-t*. The *ā* is as well elided in the 3rd person of the fem. dual when the vowelled fem. marker *-t(a)ā* is suffixed to it.

This can be illustrated in the following paragraphs.

6.5.2.1. The verb with 3rd radical w:

An example of a verb with a 3rd radical *w* is *ġazawa-t* that results in *ġaza-t* "she raided". The phonological procedure is complex as it involves more than two steps: *ġazawa-t* with the 3rd radical *w* vowelled by a fatḥa and preceded by one, becomes at first *ġaz(a)ā-t* with the *wa* changed into *ā,* and as *ġaz(a)ā-t* involves the cluster of the vowelless *ā* and *t,* it becomes *ġaza-t* with the *ā* elided.

The same principle is in operation in the dual of the 3rd person of the fem., e.g. *ġaza-t(a)ā*. It can be observed that the *ā* that is changed from the 3rd radical vowelled by a fatḥa, namely the *wa,* is as well elided in it. Hence the procedure from the base form to the derived form is the following: *ġazawa-t(a)ā* > *ġaz(a)ā-t(a)ā* > *ġaza-t(a)ā*. This elision of the *ā* is carried out in it spite of the fact that the *-t(a)ā* ending in *ġaz(a)ā-t(a)ā* that marks the fem. dual, has its *-t* vowelled by a fatḥa, implying that there does not occur a cluster of two vowelless letters which would trigger off the elision, as in the case of the 3rd person of the fem. sing. *ġaz(a)ā-t* resulting in *ġaza-t* after the necessary elision of the *ā*. However according to a theory propounded by Ibn Masᶜūd (cf. Åkesson, *Ibn Masᶜūd* 326 fol. 32a) it is assumed that there is such a combination theoretically on account that the *-t(a)* of the *-t(a)ā* that marks the fem. sing. is underlyingly vowelless, i.e. *-t,* and is only given the fatḥa when it is connected to the vowelless *-ā* suffix of the dual.

6.5.2.2. *The verb with 3rd radical y:*

The reasoning is the same as the one that is introduced concerning the verb with 3rd radical *w* (cf. par. 6.5.2.1.), except that it is the *ya* that is changed into *ā,* and then is elided. An example is *ramaya-t* "she threw" which has the 3rd radical *y* vowelled by a fatḥa and preceded by one. It becomes *ram(a)ā-t* with the *ya* changed into *ā,* and then as there is a cluster of two vowelless segments: the *ā* and *t,* its *ā* is elided so that it becomes *rama-t* (cf. Åkesson, *Ibn Masᶜūd* 326: fol. 32a).

The procedure is the same concerning the dual of the 3rd person of the fem. as the one of the verb with 3rd radical *w*. An example is *ramaya-t(a)ā* that becomes *ram(a)ā-t(a)ā* and then *rama-t(a)ā.* Some people however who use a defective dialectal variant maintain the *ā* and say *ram(a)ā-t(a)ā* instead (cf. ibid 56: fols. 5a-5b, Zamaḫšarī 154, Ibn Yaᶜīš, IX, 27-29, Wright, II, 89, Åkesson, *Conversion* 28).

6.5.3. The persons in the perfect to which the vowelled agent pronoun is suffixed to: the sequence of the 3rd vowelless weak radical preceded by a fatḥa: the retaining of the w or y:

In the forms of the perfect in which the vowelled agent pronouns are suffixed to, e.g. the *-tu* of the 1st person of the sing., the *-n(a)ā* of the 1st person of the pl., the *-ta* of the 2nd person of the masc. sing., the *-tum* of the 2nd person of the masc. pl., the *-na* of the 3rd person of the fem. pl., etc., the 3rd vowelless radical *w* or *y* is maintained.

An example of a verb with 3rd radical *w* is *ġazaw-tu* "I attacked /1st person of the sing.", *ġazaw-n(a)ā* "/1st person of the pl.", *ġazaw-ta* "/2nd person of the masc. sing.", *ġazaw-tum*

"/2nd person of the masc. pl.", *ġazaw-na* "/3rd person of the fem. pl.", etc.

An example of a verb with 3rd radical *y* is *ramay-tu* "I threw /1st person of the sing.", *ramay-n(a)ā* "/1st person of the pl.", *ramay-ta* "/2nd person of the masc. sing.", *ramay-tum* "/2nd person of the masc. pl.", *ramay-na* "/3rd person of the fem. pl.", etc.

The reason of the maintaince of the *w* or *y* in these forms is that the glide is made vowelless on account of the suffixation of the vowelled pronoun suffix of the agent, and thus is preceded by a fatḥa. The sequence of the vowelless glide preceded by a fatḥa has in most cases its glide retained.

Thus:

-aw → *-aw*

-ay → *-ay*

6.5.4. The 3rd person of the masc pl. of the perfect of the conjugation faᶜala: the sequence of the 3rd radical w or y vowelled by a ḍamma (on account that it is followed by the vowelless ū / w marker of the pl.), and preceded by a fatḥa: the change of the wu or yu into an ā and the elision of the ā:

The verb with 3rd radical *w* or *y* of the conjugation *faᶜala* that occurs in the 3rd person of the masc. pl., has the vowelless agent pronoun marking the pl., namely the *-ū,* suffixed to it, and hence has its 3rd radical vowelled with a ḍamma. The vowelled 3rd radical *w* or *y* that is preceded by a fatḥa is changed into an *ā* and the *ā* is then elided.

Thus:

-awu → *-(a)ā*

-ayu → *-(a)ā*

An example of a verb with 3rd radical *w* is *ġazaw(u)-ū* that becomes *ġaza-w* "they attacked". The procedure is the following: *ġazaw(u)-ū* / *ġazaw(u)-w* with the 3rd radical *w* vowelled by a ḍamma and preceded by a fatḥa becomes *ġaz(a)ā-w* after that the *w(u)* is changed into an *ā*. As there is a cluster of the vowelless *ā* and *w* in it, the *ā* is elided so that it becomes *ġaza-w*.

An example of a verb with 3rd radical *y* is *ramay(u)-w* that becomes *rama-w* "they threw" (cf. Åkesson, *Ibn Masᶜūd* 326: fol. 32a). The procedure is the following: *ramay(u)-w* with the 3rd radical *y* vowelled by a ḍamma and preceded by a fatḥa becomes *ram(a)ā-w* after that the *y(u)* is changed into an *ā*. As there is a cluster of the vowelless *ā* and *w* in it, the *ā* is elided so that it becomes *rama-w*.

6.5.5. The 3rd person of the masc pl. of the perfect of a verb with 3rd radical y of the conjugation faᶜila: the sequence of the 3rd radical y vowelled by a ḍamma (on account of the vowelless ū / w marker of the pl. following it), and preceded by a kasra: the transfer of the ḍamma before the y and hence the change of the kasra into a ḍamma, the elision of the y and the lengthening of the ḍamma into ū according to a theory, or the elision of the y's ḍamma, the elision of the y and the change of the kasra into a ḍamma according to another theory:

In the case of the 3rd person of the masc. pl. of the verb with 3rd radical *y* of the conjugation *faᶜila,* e.g. *raḍiya* "to consent" to which the vowelless agent pronoun namely the *-ū,* is suffixed to, namely *raḍiy(u)-ū,* the 3rd radical *y* is elided (for discussions see Wright, II, 89) resulting in *raḍi(u)-ū,* except that the 2nd radical *ḍ* becomes vowelled with a ḍamma, namely *raḍ(u)-ū,* to hinder the combination of the ḍamma followed by the kasra (cf. Åkesson, *Ibn Masᶜūd* 326: fol. 32a), which is deemed as heavy, and also so that the ḍamma accords with the suffixed *ū* (cf. Daqr, *Muᶜǧam* 390-391).

The phonological procedure is carried out by eliding the 3rd weak radical and changing the vowel of the 2nd radical into another. There exist two different theories concerning the phonological procedure resulting in the vowelling of the 2nd radical by a ḍamma.

According to the theory of Ibn Ǧinnī, *Munṣif II,* 126, *raḍiy(u)-ū* with the 3rd radical *y* vowelled by a ḍamma and preceded by a kasra becomes *raḍuy-ū* after that the ḍamma of the *y* is shifted to the segment preceding it, the *ḍ,* for the sake of alleviation, which implies that the *ḍ's* kasra is changed into a ḍamma. As there is in it a cluster of a vowelless *y* and *ū,* the *y* is elided so that it becomes *raḍ(u)-ū.*

According to the theory of Ibn Masᶜūd (cf. Åkesson, *Ibn Masᶜūd* 286: fol. 28b), there does not forecome any transfer of the ḍamma of the *y* of *raḍiy(u)-ū* to the segment before it, but the ḍamma is however elided for the sake of alleviation, namely *raḍiy-ū,* then the vowelless *y* is elided to hinder the cluster of two vowelless segments, the *y* and the *ū,* namely *raḍi-ū,* and then the *ḍ's* kasra is changed into a ḍamma resulting in *raḍ(u)-ū.*

6.5.6. The persons in which no suffix is attached to the imperfect: the sequence in which the glide is vowelled by the ḍamma of the indicative and preceded by a vowel: the elision of the ḍamma:

In the cases of the verb with 3rd *w* or *y* radical in the persons to which no suffix is attached to, as the 1st person of the sing., e.g. *ᵓaġzuwu* "I attack" with 3rd radical *w, ᵓarmiyu* "I throw" with 3rd radical *y,* the 1st person of the pl., e.g. *naġzuwu* "we attack", *narmiyu* "we throw", the 2nd person of the masc. sing., e.g. *taġzuwu* "you attack", *tarmiyu* "you throw" and the 3rd person of the fem. sing., e.g. *taġzuwu* "she attacks", *tarmiyu* "she throws", the ḍamma of the indicative that vowels the 3rd radical is elided because it is considered as heavy on the *w* or *y* (cf. Åkesson, *Ibn Masᶜūd* 326: fol. 32b). The phonological changes can be illustrated as follows:

Concerning the verb with 3rd radical *w*, the case of *yaġzuwu,* which has the *w* vowelled by a ḍamma and preceded by one, can be taken up. It becomes *yaġzuw* > *yaġz(u)ū* after the elision of the ḍamma and the assimilation of the *w* to the ḍamma resulting in the lengthened *w: ū.*

Concerning the verb with 3rd radical *y,* the case of *yarmiyu,* which has the *y* vowelled by a ḍamma and preceded by a kasra, can be taken up. It becomes *yarmiy* > *yarm(i)ī* after the elision of the ḍamma and the assimilation of the *y* to the kasra resulting in the lengthened *y: ī.*

6.5.7. The duals of the imperfect: the sequence in which the glide is vowelled by a fatḥa and preceded by a vowel: the glide's retaining:

The weak radical of the verb with 3rd radical *w* or *y* is maintained in the cases of the duals of the 2nd persons, e.g. *taġzuw(a)-āni* "you raid /2nd dual", *tarmiy(a)-āni* "you throw /2nd dual" and the 3rd persons of the pl., e.g. *yaġzuw(a)-āni* "/3 masc. dual" and *yarmiy(a)-āni* "/3 masc. dual". As for the reason of its retaining, it is because the fatḥa that vowels the glide and precedes the infix *-ā* of the dual is counted as light (cf. Åkesson, *Ibn Mas^cūd* 326: fol. 32b).

6.5.8. The 2nd person of the fem. sing. of the imperfect of a verb with 3rd radical y: the sequence in which the 3rd radical y is vowelled by a kasra and is followed by the vowelless ī marker of the fem. sing.: the elision of the vowel of the y together with the y:

The underlying form of the 2nd person of the imperfect sing. of a verb with 3rd weak radical *y*, e.g. *ramaya* "to throw" is *tarmiy(i)-īna* "/2 fem. sing.". The phonological changes are carried out in the following manner (cf. Åkesson, *Ibn Mas^cūd* 286: fol. 28b): *tarmiy(i)-īna* with the 3rd radical *y* vowelled by a kasra and preceded by one becomes *tarmiy-īna* after the elision of the kasra of the 3rd weak radical *y* due to the heaviness of the combination. As there is in it a cluster of two vowelless segments: the *y* and the *ī*, the 3rd radical *y* is elided so that it becomes *tarm(i)-īna.*

This elision of the weak 3rd radical is usual in the defective verb in which the agent pronoun of the 2nd person of the fem. sing. of the imperfect, *-īna,* is suffixed to (cf. Wright, II, 89, Daqr, *Mu^cǧam* 391).

6.5.9. The 2nd and 3rd persons of the masc. pl. of the imperfect of a verb with 3rd radical y: the sequence in which the 3rd radical y is vowelled by a ḍamma, preceded by a kasra and followed by the vowelless ū marker of the masc. pl.: the elision of the ḍamma of the y together with the y and the change of the kasra into a ḍamma:

The underlying form of the 2nd person of the imperfect sing. of a verb with 3rd weak radical *y*, e.g. *ramaya* "to throw" is *tarmiy(u)-ūna* "/2 masc. pl." and of the 3rd person of the masc. pl. *yarmiy(u)-ūna* "/3 masc. pl." The phonological changes in them both are carried out by eliding the ḍamma of the 3rd weak radical *y* due to the heaviness of the combination, namely *tarmiy-ūna* and *yarmiy-ūna.* As there results a cluster of two vowelless segments: the *y* and the *ū,* the *y* is elided and then the kasra is changed into a ḍamma to prevent that the *ū* is changed into a *y* due to its sukūn and the influence of the kasra preceding it, so they became *tarm(u)-ūna* and *yarm(u)-ūna.*

6.5.10. Form IV and other derived forms of the perfect of verbs with 3rd w radical to which the vowelled agent pronoun is suffixed to: the sequence of the 3rd vowelless weak radical preceded by a fatḥa: the change of the w into a y:

An example of a Form IV of a verb with 3rd radical *w* is *ʾaġzaw-tu* that occurs in the perfect with the pronoun of the agent suffixed to it, which becomes *ʾaġzay-tu* "I raided". The procedure is the following: *ʾaġzaw-tu* with the vowelless 3rd radical *w* preceded by a fatḥa becomes *ʾaġzay-tu* after that the *w* is changed into a *y*.

This change of the *w* into a *y* is on the analogy of the one that is carried out in its imperfect *yuġziwu* > *yuġz(i)yu* > *yuġz(i)ī* "he raids" (cf. Åkesson, *Ibn Masʿūd* 282: 27a; and for discussions see 6.5.11.).

Some other examples of derived forms in which this phonological change is carried out on the analogy of the one that is carried out in their imperfects, are Form II *ġazzawa* that becomes *ġazzaya* and then *ġazz(a)ā* [with final *alif maqṣūra]* "to raid" and Form X *ʾistarḍawa* that becomes *ʾistarḍaya* and then *ʾistarḍ(a)ā* "to consent" (cf. Wright, II, 91).

6.5.11. Form IV and other derived forms of the imperfect of the verbs with 3rd w radical: the sequence of the 3rd vowelled weak radical preceded by a kasra: the change of the w into a y:

An example of a Form IV of a verb with 2nd radical *w* in the imperfect is *yuġziwu* in which the vowelled *w* is preceded by a kasra which is why it is changed into a *y*, namely *yuġz(i)yu* that becomes *yuġz(i)ī* "he raids". The procedure is the following: *yuġziwu* with the vowelless 3rd radical *w* preceded by a kasra becomes *yuġz(i)yu* after that the *w* is changed into a *y*. As in it the *y* is preceded by a kasra and vowelled by a ḍamma, the *y's* ḍamma is elided and the *y* is assimilated to the kasra resulting in the lengthened *y*: *ī*, so that it becomes *yuġz(i)ī*.

Some other examples of derived forms in which this phonological change is carried out are Form II *yuġazziwu* that becomes *yuġazziyu* "he raids" and then *yuġazz(i)ī* and Form X *yastarḍiwu* that becomes *yastarḍiyu* and then *yastarḍ(i)ī*.

6.5.12. The active participle of the verb with 3rd radical y: the sequence of the vowelled y preceded by a kasra in the definite and indefinite forms: the elision of the vowel of the y in the definite form, and the elision of the vowel together with the 3rd radical y in the nominative and genitive cases with the tanwīn replacing the kasra of the 2nd radical in the indefinite form:

The active participle's form of verbs with *w* and *y* 3rd radical is *f(a)ā^{c}ilun*. An example of an active participle with 3rd radical *y* in the definite form of the underlying form is *al-r(a)ām(i)yu* "the one who throws" that becomes *al-r(a)ām(i)ī* in the cases of the nominative, accusative and genitive with the vowelless *ī*, because of the dislike of vowelling the *y* after the kasra. Its underlying form as an indefinite noun is *r(a)āmiyun* for the nominative and *r(a)āmiyin* for the genetive. The 3rd radical together with the vowel is elided and the *tanwīn* replaces the kasra of 2nd radical, namely *r(a)āmin* which is used for both the nominative and the genitive (cf. Åkesson, *Ibn Mas*ᶜ*ūd* 328: fol 33a, Wright, II, 90). The reason why the *y* is made vowelless and is then elided in both these cases is the heaviness of both the ḍamma and the kasra vowelling it. It is not elided in the accusative *r(a)āmiyan* because the nunation with the fatḥa is considered as light.

6.5.13. The passive participle of the verb with 3rd radical y: the sequence of the vowelless infixed ū preceding the y: the change of the vowelless infixed ū into a y, the change of the ḍamma preceding the changed y into a kasra and the assimilation of the y to the y:

The passive participle of verbs with 3rd radical *y* is formed according to *maf*ᶜ*(u)wlun / maf*ᶜ*(u)ūlun.* An example is the underlying form *marm(u)wyun / marm(u)ūyun* that becomes *marmiyyun* "what is thrown" (cf. Åkesson, *Ibn Mas*ᶜ*ūd* 328: fol 33a, Howell, IV, fasc. I, 1543, de Sacy, I, 108, Wright, II, 91, Vernier, I 340-341). The procedure is the following: *marm(u)wyun / marm(u)ūyun* with the vowelless infixed *w / ū* preceding the *y* and preceded by a ḍamma becomes *marm(u)yyun* after that the *w* is changed into a *y* due to the *y's* influence. As there is in it a heavy combination of a ḍamma preceding the yāʾs, the ḍamma is changed into a kasra so that it becomes *marm(i)yyun.*

6.5.14. The noun of place of the verb with 3rd radical y: the sequence of the vowelled y preceded by a kasra: the change of the kasra into a fatḥa and of the y into an alif maqṣūra:

The pattern of the noun of place of the verb with 3rd radical *y* is *mafʿalun* and not *mafʿilun* (cf. Åkesson, *Ibn Masʿūd* 88: fol. 17a, Zamaḫšarī, 104, Wright, II, 127-128, Vernier, I, 188). The reason why the kasra is changed into a fatḥa is to avoid having a vowelled *y* following a kasra that is deemed as heavy. Hence *al-marmiyu* becomes *al-marm(a)ā* "a place of throwing or shooting arrows", with the kasra of the *m* changed into a fatḥa and the *y* changed into an *alif maqṣūra.*

6.5.15. The jussive of the verb with 3rd radical w or y: the sequence of the vowelless w or y preceded by a vowel: the elision of the w or y:

As a rule the 3rd radical *w* or *y* of the verb that takes the sukūn as a marker of the jussive mood is elided (cf. Åkesson, *Ibn Masʿūd* 328: fol 32b).

The reason of this elision is that the weak 3rd radical holds the same position as the vowel of the strong verb. As the strong verb's 3rd radical loses its vowel and takes the sukūn as a marker of the jussive mood, e.g. *lam yaḍrib* "he did not hit", the verb with weak 3rd radical loses its weak radical, e.g. *lam yaġzu* that is said instead of *lam yaġz(u)ū* "he did not attack" and *lam yarmi* that is said instead of *lam yarm(i)ī* "he did not throw".

6.6. A few remarks concerning some homonymous forms

An example that applies for both the 3rd person of the masc. sing. and the 3rd person of the fem. pl. is *yaᶜf(u)ūna* "he remits it, or they remit it /fem. pl., respectively", from *ᶜaf(a)ā* [with final alif mamdūda] underlyingly *ᶜafawa* "to be obliterated", a verb with 3rd *w* radical. It is only by referring to the underlying forms of the intended persons that it possible to differenciate them from each other (cf. Åkesson, *Ibn Masᶜūd* 326: fol. 32b).

The underlying form of the 3rd person of the masc. pl. is *yaᶜfuw(u)-ūna* (formed according to *yafᶜul(u)-ūna)* of which the 3rd radical *w* vowelled by a ḍamma is elided on account of the suffixation of the vowelless agent marker of the masc. pl., the *ū*, preceding the *-na* of the indicative, resulting in *yaᶜf(u)-ūna.*

The underlying form of the 3rd person of the fem. pl. is *yaᶜf(u)w-na* > *yaᶜf(u)ū-na* (formed according to *yafᶜul-na)* with the 3rd radical *w* maintained before the suffix marker of the fem. pl., the *-na.*

The *-na,* marker of the indicative in the ending *-ūna,* is dropped in the 3rd person of the masc. pl. in the case of the subjunctive in the sur. 2: 237 *(wa-ᵓan taᶜfū ᵓaqrabu li-l-taqwā)* "And the remission (of the man's half) is the nearest to righteousness" (cf. Howell, II-III, 16-17), in which *wa-ᵓan taᶜf(u)-ū* is said instead *wa-ᵓan taᶜf(u)-ūna,* and so as well in the case of the jussive, e.g. *lam taᶜf(u)-ū* "you did not remit" as a marker for these moods.

The *-na,* marker of the fem. pl., is not dropped in the sur. 2: 237 *(ᵓillā ᵓan yaᶜfūna)* "Unless they remit it" (cf. Åkesson, *Ibn Masᶜūd* 326: fol. 32b), as the *-na* in *yaᶜf(u)ū-na* is not the marker of the indicative that is elided in the subjunctive mood, but the marker of the fem. pl.

7. THE VERB THAT IS DOUBLY WEAK

The verb that is doubly weak is named *al-lafīf* "complicated, tangled".

It is divided into two classes:

1- *mafrūq:* having a 1st and 3rd weak radical, e.g. *waq(a)ā yaq(i)y* "to guard, preserve".

2- *maqrūn:* having a 2nd and 3rd weak radical, e.g. *ṭaw(a)ā yaṭw(i)y* "to fold".

7.1. The conjugations of the verb with 1st and 3rd weak radical

The verb with 1st and 3rd weak radical falls into the following conjugations:

1- *fa^{c}ala yaf^{c}ilu,* e.g. *waqaya yaqiyu* that becomes after the phonological change *waq(a)ā* [with final *alif maqṣūra] yaq(i)ī* "to guard, preserve".

2- *fa^{c}ila yaf^{c}ilu,* e.g. *waliya yaliyu* "to be near" of which only the imperfect becomes after the phonological change *yal(i)ī.*

3- *fa^{c}ila yaf^{c}alu,* e.g. *wağiya yawğayu* of which only the imperfect becomes after the phonological change *yawğ(a)ā* [with final *alif maqṣūra].*

7.2. Examples of some derivatives and paradigms of the verb with 1st and 3rd weak radical

An example of a verb with 1st and 3rd weak radical in the perfect is *waq(a)ā* "he guarded". It becomes *yaqī* in the imperfect of the indicative active. Its imperative is *qi* or *qih,* its active participle is *wāqin,* its *maṣdar* is *waqyun,* its perfect passive is *wuqiya,* its imperfect is *yūqā,* its passive participle is *mawqīyun,* its noun of place is *mawqan* and its noun of instrument is *mīqan.*

Its paradigm in the perfect, active, is as follows:

	sing.	dual	pl.
1st	*waqay-tu*		*waqay-n(a)ā*
2nd masc.	*waqay-ta*	*waqay-tum(a)ā*	*waqay-tum*
2nd fem.	*waqay-ti*	*waqay-tum(a)ā*	*waqa-tunna*
3rd masc.	*waq(a)ā*	*waq(a)-ā*	*waqa-w*
3rd fem.	*waqa-t*	*waqa-t(a)ā*	*waqay-na*

Its imperfect in the indicative, active, is the following:

	sing.	dual	pl.
1st	*ʾaq(i)ī*		*naq(i)ī*
2nd masc.	*taq(i)ī*	*taqiy(a)-āni*	*taq(u)-ūna*
2nd fem.	*taq(i)-īna*	*taqiy(a)-āni*	*taq(i)-īna*
3rd masc.	*yaq(i)ī*	*yaqiy(a)-āni*	*yaq(u)-ūna*
3rd fem.	*taq(i)ī*	*taqiy(a)-āni*	*yaq(i)-īna*

Its imperfect in the indicative, subjunctive, is the following:

	sing.	dual	pl.
1st	*ʾaq(i)ya*		*naq(i)ya*
2nd masc.	*taq(i)ya*	*taqiy(a)-ā*	*taq(u)-ū*
2nd fem.	*taq(i)ya*	*taqiy(a)-ā*	*taq(i)-īna*
3rd masc.	*yaq(i)ya*	*yaqiy(a)-ā*	*yaq(u)-ū*
3rd fem.	*taq(i)ya*	*taqiy(a)-ā*	*yaq(i)-īna*

Its imperfect in the indicative, jussive, is the following:

	sing.	dual	pl.
1st	*ʾaqi*		*naqi*
2nd masc.	*taqi*	*taqiy(a)-ā*	*taq(u)-ū*
2nd fem.	*taq(i)-ī*	*taqiy(a)-ā*	*taq(i)-īna*
3rd masc.	*yaqi*	*yaqiy(a)-ā*	*yaq(u)-ū*
3rd fem.	*taqi*	*taqiy(a)-ā*	*yaq(i)-īna*

7.2.1. Remarks concerning the phonological procedures in some of its forms:

The 1st weak radical of the verb with 1st and 3rd weak radical is submitted to the same rules as the 1st weak radical of the verb with 1st radical *w* or *y* and its 3rd weak radical is submitted to the same rules as the 3rd weak radical of the verb with 3rd radical *w* or *y*.

7.3. The conjugations of the verb with 1st and 3rd weak radical

The verb with 2nd and 3rd weak radical falls into the following conjugations:

1- *faᶜala yafᶜilu,* e.g. *ṭawaya yaṭwiyu* that becomes after the phonological change ṭawā [with final *alif maqṣūra] yaṭwī* "to fold".

2- *faᶜila yafᶜalu,* e.g. *qawiya yaqwayu* "to be strong" of which only the imperfect becomes after the phonological change *yaqwā* [with final *alif maqṣūra].*

3- *faᶜila yafᶜalu,* e.g. *ḥayiya yaḥyayu* of which only the imperfect becomes after the phonological change *yaḥyā* [with final *alif mamdūda].*

7.4. Examples of some derivatives and paradigms of the verb with 2nd and 3rd weak radical

An example of a verb with 2nd and 3rd weak radical in the perfect is *ṭawā* [with final *alif maqṣūra]* "he folded". It becomes *yaṭwī* in the imperfect of the indicative active. Its imperative is *ʾiṭwi,* its active participle is *ṭāwin,* its *maṣdar* is *ṭayyun,* its perfect passive is *ṭuwiya,* its imperfect is *yuṭwā,* its passive participle is *maṭwīyun,* its noun of place is *maṭwan* and its noun of instrument is *miṭwan.*

Its paradigm in the perfect, active, is as follows:

	sing.	dual	pl.
1st	*ṭaway-tu*		*ṭaway-n(a)ā*
2nd masc.	*ṭaway-ta*	*ṭaway-tum(a)ā*	*ṭaway-tum*
2nd fem.	*ṭaway-ti*	*ṭaway-tum(a)ā*	*ṭaway-tunna*
3rd masc.	*ṭaw(a)ā*	*ṭaw(a)-ā*	*ṭawa-w*
3rd fem.	*ṭawa-t*	*ṭawa-t(a)ā*	*ṭaway-na*

Its imperfect in the indicative, active, is the following:

	sing.	dual	pl.
1st	*ʾaṭw(i)ī*		*naṭw(i)ī*
2nd masc.	*taṭw(i)ī*	*taṭwiy(a)-āni*	*taṭw(u)-ūna*
2nd fem.	*taṭw(i)-īna*	*taṭwiy(a)-āni*	*taṭw(i)-īna*
3rd masc.	*yaṭw(i)ī*	*yaṭwiy(a)-āni*	*yaṭw(u)-ūna*
3rd fem.	*taṭw(i)ī*	*taṭwiy(a)-āni*	*yaṭw(i)-īna*

Its imperfect in the indicative, subjunctive, is the following:

	sing.	dual	pl.
1st	*ʾaṭw(i)ya*		*naṭw(i)ya*
2nd masc.	*taṭw(i)ya*	*taṭwiy(a)-ā*	*tatw(u)-ū*
2nd fem.	*taṭw(i)ya*	*taṭwiy(a)-ā*	*tatw(i)-īna*
3rd masc.	*yaṭw(i)ya*	*yaṭwiy(a)-ā*	*yaṭw(u)-ū*
3rd fem.	*taṭw(i)ya*	*taṭwiy(a)-ā*	*yaṭw(i)-īna*

Its imperfect in the indicative, jussive, is the following:

	sing.	dual	pl.
1st	*ʾaṭwi*		*naṭwi*
2nd masc.	*taṭwi*	*taṭwiy(a)-ā*	*taṭw(u)-ū*
2nd fem.	*taṭw(i)-ī*	*taṭwiy(a)-ā*	*taṭw(i)-īna*
3rd masc.	*yaṭwi*	*yaṭwiy(a)-ā*	*yaṭw(u)-ū*
3rd fem.	*taṭwi*	*taṭwiy(a)-ā*	*yaṭw(i)-īna*

7.4.1. Remarks concerning the phonological procedures in some of its forms:

The 2nd weak radical of the verb with 2nd and 3rd weak radical is submitted to the same rules as the 2nd weak radical of the verb with 2nd radical *w* or *y* and its 3rd weak radical is submitted to the same rules as the 3rd weak radical of the verb with 3rd radical *w* or *y*.

8. BIBLIOGRAPHY

8.1. Primary sources

ᶜAbd al-Ḥamīḍ, *Taṣrīf* = ᶜAbd al-Ḥamīd, M. Muḥyī l-Dīn, *Takmila fī Taṣrīf al-afᶜāl,* the work printed after Ibn ᶜAqīl, Šarḥ II.

ᶜAbd al-Raḥīm, *Ṣarf* = ᶜAbd al-Raḥīm, Saᶜd, *Muqaddamat fī ᶜilm al-ṣarf,* Cairo s.a.

Åkesson, *Ibn Masᶜūd* = Åkesson, J. , *Arabic Morphology and Phonology based on the Marāḥ al-arwāḥ by Aḥmad b. ᶜAlī b. Masᶜūd, Presented with an Introduction, Arabic Edition, English Translation and Commentary,* Leiden 2001.

Astarābāḏī, *Šarḥ al-šāfiya* = Al-Astarābāḏī, Raḍī l-Dīn Muḥammad b. al-Ḥasan, *Šarḥ šāfiyat Ibn al-Ḥāğib,* edited with *Šarḥ šawāhid* written by ᶜAbd al-Qādir al-Baġdādī, 4 vol., Beirut 1395/1975.

Bakkūš, *Taṣrif* = Al-Bakkūš, Ṭ., *al-Taṣrif al-ᶜarabī,* Tunis 1973.

Bustānī, *Muḥīṭ* = Al-Bustānī, B., *Muḥīṭ al-muḥīṭ,* an Arabic-Arabic Dictionary, Libanon 1983.

Carter, *Linguistics [Širbīnī, Āğurrūmīya]* = Carter, M. G., *Arab Linguistics, an introductory classical text with translation and notes,* Amsterdam 1981.

Daqr, *Muᶜğam* = Daqr, ᶜAbd al-Ġanī, *Muᶜğam al-naḥw,* Beirut 1407 A.H. /1986.

Farrāᵓ, *Maᶜānī* = Farrāᵓ, Abū Zakarīya Yaḥyā b. Ziyād, *Maᶜānī l-qurᵓān,* 3 vol., Ed. M. Y. Nağatī and M. ᶜA. Naǧǧār, Cairo 1955-1972.

Freytag, *Proverbia* = Freytag, G. W., *Arabum Proverbia,* T. I. II. III, I. II. Bonnae 1838-43.

Ḥadīṯī, *Nuḥāt* = Al-Ḥadīṯī, Ḫadīğa, *Mawqif al-nuḥāt mina l-iḥtiğāğ bi-l-ḥadīṯ,* Irak 1986.

Ḫalīl b. Aḥmad..., *Ḥurūf* = Ḫalīl b. Aḥmad wa-b. al-Sakīt wa-l-Rāzī, *Ṯalāṯat kutub fī l-ḥurūf,* Ed. R. ᶜAbd al-Tawwāb, Cairo 1982.

Ibn al-Anbārī, *Inṣāf* = Ibn al-Anbārī, Abū l-Barakāt, *Kitāb al-inṣāf fī masāʾil al-ḫilāf bayna l-naḥwīyīn al-baṣrīyīn wa-l-kūfīyīn: Die grammatischen Schulen von Kufa und Basra,* Ed. G. Weil, Leiden 1913.

Ibn al-Anbārī, *Asrār* = Ibn al-Anbārī, Abū l-Barakāt, *Asrār al-ᶜarabīya,* Ed. B. al-Bayṭār, Damascus 1377/1957.

Ibn ᶜAqīl = Ibn ᶜAqīl, *Bihāʾ al-Dīn ᶜAbdallāh,* ˇ*Šarḥ ᶜalā alfīyat Ibn Mālik,* Ed. ᶜA. al-Ḥamīd, 2 vol., undated.

Ibn Fāris, *Ṣāḥibī* = Ibn Fāris, Aḥmad, *al-Ṣāḥibī fī fiqh al-luġa wa-sanan al-ᶜarab fī kalāmihā,* Ed. M. al-Chouémi, (bibliotheca Philologica; I), Beyrouth 1382/1963.

Ibn Ǧinnī, *de Flexione* = Ibn Ǧinnîi, Abū l-Fatḥ ᶜUṯmān, *de Flexione Libellvs,* Ed. G. Hoberg, Lipsiae, 1885.

Ibn Ǧinnī, *Ḫaṣāʾiṣ* = Ibn Ǧinnī, Abū l-Fatḥ ᶜUṯmān, *al-Ḫaṣāʾiṣ,* Ed. M. A. al-Naǧǧār, 3 vol., Cairo 1371/1952-1376/1956.

Ibn Ǧinnī, *Munṣif* = Ibn Ǧinnī, Abū l-Fatḥ ᶜUṯmān, *al-Munṣif fī šarḥ taṣrīf al-Māzinī,* Ed. I. Muṣṭafā, ᶜA. Amīn, 3 vol., Cairo 1373/1954-1379/1960.

Ibn Ǧinnī, *Sirr* = Ibn Ǧinnī, Abū l-Fatḥ ᶜUṯmān, *Sirr ṣināᶜat al-iᶜrāb,* Ed. Ḥ. Hindāwī, 2 vol., Damascus 1405/1985.

Ibn Ḫālawaihi, *Iᶜrāb* = Ibn Ḫālawiya, Abū ᶜAbd Allāh al-Ḥusain b. Aḥmad, *Iᶜrāb ṯalāt–īn sūra mina l-Qurᵓān,* Damascus s.a.

Ibn Ḫālawaihi, *Qirāᵓāt* = Ibn Ḫālawaihi, Abū ᶜAbd Allāh al-Ḥusain b. Aḥmad, *Iᶜrāb al-qirāᵓāt al-sabᶜ wa-ᶜilaluhā,* Ed. ᶜAbd al-Raḥmān b. Sulaimān al-ᶜAtīmain, 2 vol., Cairo 1413/1992.

Ibn Mālik, *La Alfīya* = Ibn Mālik, Muḥammad b. ᶜAbd Allāh, *La ᵓAlfiyyah d'Ibnu-Malik* [pp. 1-227], suivie de (->) *La Lāmiyyah* du meme auteur (pp. 228-353) avec traduction et notes en français et un lexique des termes techniques par A. Goguyer, Beyrouth 1888.

Ibn Manẓūr = Ibn Manẓūr, Ǧamāl al-Dīn, *Lisān al-ᶜArab,* 6 vol., Beirut undated.

Ibn al-Sarrāǧ, *ᵓUṣūl* = Ibn al-Sarrāǧ, Abū Bakr, *al-ᵓUṣūl fī l-Naḥw,* Ed. ᶜA. Ḥ. al-Fatlī, Beirut 1408/1988.

Ibn ᶜUṣfūr = Ibn ᶜUṣfūr al-Ašbīlī, Abū l-ᶜAbbās ᶜAlī b. Muʾmin, *al-Mumtiᶜ fī l-taṣrīf,* Ed. F. al-Dīn Qabāwih, Aleppo 1390/1970.

Ibn Yaᶜīš = Ibn Yaᶜīš, Muwaffaq al-Dīn Abū l-Barāʾ Yaᶜīš, *Šarḥ al-mufaṣṣal,* 2 vol., Beirut undated.

Ibn Yaᶜīš, *Mulūkī* = Ibn Yaᶜīš, Muwaffaq al-Dīn Abū l-Barāʾ Yaᶜīš, *Šarḥ al-mulūkī fī l-taṣrīf,* Ed. Faḫr al-Dīn Qabāwa, Aleppo 1393/1973.

Maḫzūmī, *Naḥw* = Al-Maḫzūmī, M., *Fī l-naḥw al-ᶜarabī,* Beirut 1986.

Muʾaddib, *Taṣrīf* = Al-Muʾaddib, al-Qāsim b. Muḥammad b. Saᶜīd, *Daqāʾiq al-taṣrīf,* Ed. A. N. al-Qaisī, Ḥ. Ṣ. al-Ḍāmin and Ḥ. Tūrāl, Iraq 1407/1987.

Rāǧiḥī, *Farrāʾ* = Al-Rāǧiḥī, Šaraf al-Dīn, *Fī l-muṣṭalaḥ al-ṣarfī ᶜinda l-Farrāʾfī kitābati "Maᶜānī l-qurʾān",* Alexandria 1992.

Sībawaihi = Sîbawaihi, Abū Bišr ᶜAmr b. ᶜUṯmān, *Le Livre de Sîbawaihi (Kitāb Sībawaihi), Traité de grammaire arabe,* Ed. H. Derenbourg, 2 vol., Paris 1881-1889. Réimpression: 1970.

Širbīnī, *Āğurrūmīya* = see Carter, *Linguistics*.

Suyūṭī, *Ašbāh* = Al-Suyūṭī, Ğalāl al-Dīn Abū l-Faḍl ᶜAbd al-Raḥmān, *al-ᵓAšbāh wa-l-naẓāᵓir*, Ed. ᶜAbd Allāh Nabhān, 4 vol., Damascus 1406/1985.

Suyūṭī, *Muzhir* = Al-Suyūṭī, Ğalāl al-Dīn Abū l-Faḍl ᶜAbd al-Raḥmān, *al-Muzhir fī ᶜulūm al-luġa wa-anwāᶜihā*, 2 vol., Cairo undated.

Ṯaᶜlab, *Mağālis* = Ṯaᶜlab, Abū l-ᶜAbbās Aḥmad b. Yaḥyā, *Mağālis*, Ed. ᶜA. al-Salām Hārūn, 1375/1956.

ᶜUkbarī, *Masāᵓil* = Al-ᶜUkbarī, Abd Allāh b. al-Ḥusain, *Masāᵓil ḫilāfīya fī l-naḥw*, Ed. M. Ḫ. al-Ḥalawānī, Aleppo, undated.

Versteegh, *Zağğāğī* = Versteegh, K., *The explanation of linguistic causes. Az-Zağğāğī's theory of grammar. Introduction, translation, commentary*, Amsterdam 1995.

Zabīdī, *Tāğ* = Al-Zabīdī, Muḥammad b. Muḥammad Murtaḍā l-Ḥusainī, *Tāğ al-ᶜarūs min ğawāhir al-qāmūs*, Ed. M. Ḥiğāzī, Kuweit 1369/1969.

Zağğāğī, *Īḍāḥ* = Al-Zağğāğī, Abū Qāsim ᶜAbd al-Raḥmān, *al-Īḍāḥ fī ᶜilal al-naḥw*, Ed. M. al-Mubārak, Cairo 1378/1959.

Zamaḫšarī = Zamaḫs'ario, Abū l-Qāsim Maḥmūd b. ᶜUmar, *al-Mufaṣṣal,* Ed. J. P. Broch, Christianiae 1840.

8.2. Secondary sources

Åkesson, *Conversion* = Åkesson, J., *Conversion of the yāʾ into an alif in Classical Arabic* in: ZAL 31, Wiesbaden 1996.

Åkesson, *Elision* = Åkesson, *Anomalous elision and addition of a vowel in Classical Arabic,* in: ZAL 36, Wiesbaden 1999.

Åkesson, *Ibn Masᶜūd* = Åkesson, J., *Arabic Morphology and Phonology based on the Marāḥ al-arwāḥ by Aḥmad b. ᶜAlī b. Masᶜūd, Presented with an Introduction, Arabic Edition, English Translation and Commentary,* Leiden 2001.

Blachère = Blachère, R., et Gaudefroy-Demombynes, M., *Grammaire de l'Arabe classique,* Paris, 1952.

Bohas/Kouloughli, *Linguistic* = Bohas, G., Guillaume, J.-P., Kouloughli, D.E., *The Arabic Linguistic Tradition,* London and New York 1990.

Carter, *Linguistics* [Širbīnī, *Āǧurrūmīya]* = Carter, M. G., *Arab Linguistics, an introductory classical text with translation and notes,* Amsterdam 1981.

Fleisch, *Traité I* = Fleisch, H., *Traité de Philologie Arabe, vol. I, Préliminaires, Phonétique Morphologie Nominale,* Beyrouth 1961.

Fleisch, *Traité II* = Fleisch, H., *Traité de Philologie Arabe, vol. II, Pronoms, Morphologie verbale, Particules,* Beyrouth 1979.

Fleischer, *Beiträge* = Fleischer, H. O., *Beiträge zur arabischen Sprachkunde,* - in: Berichte der k. sächs. Ges. d. Wiss. Philol.-hist. Cl. I, 1863, pp. 93-176.

- " " (Fortsetzung.) Ibid., II, 1864, pp. 265-326.

- " " - " III, 1866, pp. 286-342.

- " " - " IV, 1870, pp. 227-295.

- " " - " V, 1874, pp. 71-158.

- " " - " VI, 1876, pp. 44-109.

- " " - " VII, 1878, pp. 65-146.

Ḥassān, *Uṣūl* = Ḥassān, Tammām, *al-Uṣūl,* Cairo 1982.

Haywood, *Lexicography* = Haywood, J. A., *Arabic lexicography. Its history, and its place in the general history of lexicography*, Leiden 1965.

Howell = Howell, M. S., *Grammar of the Classical Arabic Language,* 4 parts in 7 vol., Allahabad 1880-1911.

Lane = Lane, E.W., *Arabic-English Lexicon,* 8 in 2 vol., London 1863-1893. Reprint: 1984.

Owens, *Foundations* = Owens, J., *The Foundations of Grammar, An Introduction to Medieval Arabic Grammatical Theory,* Amsterdam/ Philadelphia 1988.

Penrice, *Dictionary* = Penrice, J., *A Dictionary and Glossary of the Kor-ân,* London 1873. Reprint: 1971.

Rabin = Rabin, C., *Ancient West-Arabian,* London 1951.

Roman, *Étude* = Roman, A., *Étude de la phonologie et de la morphologie de la koinè arabe,* 2 vol., Publications de l'Université de Provence, Marseille 1983.

De Sacy = De Sacy, S., *Grammaire arabe,* 2 vol., Tunis 1904-1905.

Vernier = Vernier, D., *Grammaire arabe,* 2 vol., Beyrouth 1891.

Versteegh, *Langage* = Versteegh, C. H. M., *The Arabic language,* Edinburgh 1996.

Versteegh, *Zağğāğī* = Versteegh, K., *The explanation of linguistic causes. Az-Zağğāğī's theory of grammar. Introduction, translation, commentary,* Amsterdam 1995.

Volck/Kellgren, *Ibn Mālik* = Volck, W., *Ibn Mālik's Lâmîyat al afcâl mit Badraddîn's Commentar von Kellgren,* Mémoires de l'académie impériale des sciences de St.-Petersbourg, tome VII, No 6, St. Petersburg 1864.

Vollers, *Volkssprache* = Vollers, K., *Volkssprache und Schriftsprache im alten Arabien,* Strassburg 1906.

Wright = Wright, W., *A Grammar of the Arabic Language,* Cambridge, Third Edition 1985.

Wright, *Comparative Grammar* = Wright, W., *Lectures on the Comparative Grammar of the Semitic Languages,* Cambridge 1890.

9. INDEX OF QUR'ANIC QUOTATIONS

10. INDEX OF VERSES

11. INDEX OF NAMES

12. EXTENDED TABLE OF CONTENTS

5. The class of the verb with 2nd radical w or y   *159*

substituted for the glide vowelled by a fatḥa) is followed by the -*t* that marks the fem.: the elision of the *ā:* *215*

6.5.2.1. The verb with 3rd radical *w:* *215*

6.5.2.2. The verb with 3rd radical *y:* *216*

6.5.3. The persons in the perfect to which the vowelled agent pronoun is suffixed to: the sequence of the 3rd vowelless weak radical preceded by a fatḥa: the retaining of the *w* or *y:* *217*

6.5.4. The 3rd person of the masc pl. of the perfect of the conjugation faᶜala: the sequence of the 3rd radical *w* or *y* vowelled by a ḍamma (on account that it is followed by the vowelless *ū* / *w* marker of the pl.), and preceded by a fatḥa: the change of the *wu* or *yu* into an *ā* and the elision of the *ā:* *218*

6.5.5. The 3rd person of the masc pl. of the perfect of a verb with 3rd radical *y* of the conjugation *faᶜila:* the sequence of the 3rd radical *y* vowelled by a ḍamma (on account of the vowelless *ū* / *w* marker of the pl. following it), and preceded by a kasra: the transfer of the ḍamma before the *y* and hence the change of the kasra into a ḍamma, the elision of the *y* and the lengthening of the ḍamma into *ū* according to a theory, or the elision of the *y's* ḍamma, the elision of the *y* and the change of the kasra into a ḍamma according to another theory: 220

6.5.6. The persons in which no suffix is attached to the imperfect: the sequence in which the glide is vowelled by the ḍamma of the indicative and preceded by a vowel: the elision of the ḍamma: 221

6.5.13. The passive participle of the verb with 3rd radical *y:* the sequence of the vowelless infixed *ū* preceding the *y:* the change of the vowelless infixed *ū* into a *y,* the change of the ḍamma preceding the changed *y* into a kasra and the assimilation of the *y* to the *y:* *227*

6.5.14. The noun of place of the verb with 3rd radical *y:* the sequence of the vowelled *y* preceded by a kasra: the change of the kasra into a fatḥa and of the *y* into an *alif maqṣūra:* *228*

6.5.15. The jussive of the verb with 3rd radical *w* or *y:* the sequence of the vowelless *w* or *y* preceded by a vowel: the elision of the *w* or *y:* *228*

6.6. A few remarks concerning some homonymous forms 229

7. The verb that is doubly weak 231

7.1. The conjugations of the verb with 1st and 3rd weak radical 232

7.2. Examples of some derivatives and paradigms of the verb with 1st and 3rd weak radical 232

7.2.1. Remarks concerning the phonological procedures in some of its forms: 234

7.3. The conjugations of the verb with 1st and 3rd weak radical 234

7.4. Examples of some derivatives and paradigms of the verb with 2nd and 3rd weak radical 235

www.ingramcontent.com/pod-product-compliance
Lightning Source LLC
Chambersburg PA
CBHW062152080426
42734CB00010B/1662
* 9 7 8 9 1 9 7 8 9 5 4 0 8 *